Robert Shufflebotnam

PHOTOSHOP
CS3

in easy steps

In easy steps is an imprint of Computer Step
Southfield Road · Southam
Warwickshire CV47 0FB · United Kingdom
www.ineasysteps.com

Notice of Liability
Every effort has been made to ensure that this book contains accurate
and current information. However, Computer Step and the author
shall not be liable for any loss or damage suffered by readers as a
result of any information contained herein.

Trademarks
Photoshop® is a registered trademark of Adobe Systems Incorporated.
All other trademarks are acknowledged as belonging to their
respective companies.

Printed and bound in the United Kingdom

ISBN-13 978-1-84078-343-8
ISBN-10 1-84078-343-5

Contents

9 Working with Type — 139

10 Paths — 149

11 Channels and Masks — 159

12 Color Adjustments — 169

1 Basic Theory

An understanding of the basics of color is important if you are to get the best out of Photoshop.

Bitmaps and Vectors

Photoshop is an image-editing application with a wealth of tools and commands for working on digital images or bitmaps. There are utilities for retouching, color correcting, compositing and more. There are also over 100 functional and creative filters that can be applied to entire images, selected areas, or specific layers.

A bitmap image consists of a rectangular grid, or raster, of pixels – in concept, very much like a mosaic. When you edit a bitmap you are editing the color values of individual pixels or groups of pixels.

Image-editing applications differ fundamentally from vector-based applications such as Adobe Illustrator. In these applications, you work with objects that can be moved, scaled, transformed, stacked and deleted as individual or grouped objects, but all the time each exists as a complete, separate object.

These applications are called vector drawing packages, as each object is defined by a mathematical formula. Because of this, they are resolution-independent – you can scale vector drawings up or down (either in the originating application or in a page layout application such as QuarkXPress or Adobe InDesign) and they will still print smoothly and crisply.

Don't forget

You should always try to scan an image at, or slightly larger than, the size at which you intend to use it. This means you will avoid having to increase the size of the image.

Scaled to 400%

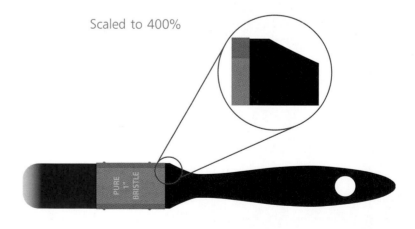

Vector drawing at actual size

...cont'd

In contrast, bitmaps are created at a set resolution – a fixed number of pixels per inch. If you scan an image at a specific resolution, then double its size, you are effectively halving its resolution (unless you add more pixels). You are likely to end up with a blocky, jagged image, as you have increased the size of the individual pixels that make up the bitmap image.

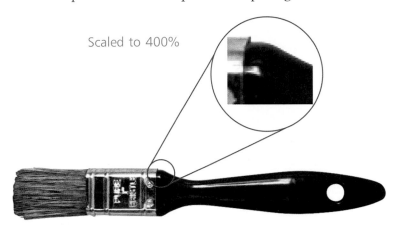

Scaled to 400%

300ppi bitmap at actual size

Bitmaps and bit-depth

An important factor when the digital data for an image is captured, typically using a digital camera or by scanning, is its bit-depth. Bit-depth refers to the amount of digital storage space used to record information about the color of a pixel. The more bits you use, the more color information you can store to describe the color of a pixel – but also, the larger the file size you end up with.

To output realistic images using PostScript technology an image should be able to represent 256 gray levels. A 24-bit scan is sufficient for recording 256 gray levels for each of the Red, Green and Blue channels (8-bits for each channel), resulting in a possible combination of over 16 million colors.

Ideally, when you work on images in Photoshop you will do so using a monitor capable of displaying over 16 million colors. This ensures that you see all the color detail in the image. Although you can work on images using only thousands of colors, for best results, especially where color reproduction is important, you need to work with as many colors as possible.

9

Pixels and Resolution

Pixels

A pixel is the smallest element in a bitmap image captured by a digital camera or a scanner. Pixel is short for "picture element". Zoom in on an image in Photoshop and you will start to see the individual pixels – the fundamental building blocks – that make up the image. When working in Photoshop, you are editing pixels, changing their color, shade and brightness.

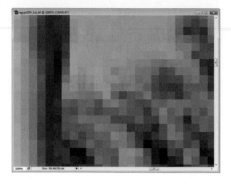

Resolution

A key factor when working on bitmap images is resolution. This is measured in pixels per inch (ppi).

Pixels can vary in size. If you have an image with a resolution of 100 ppi, each pixel would be 1/100th of an inch square. In an image with a resolution of 300 ppi, each pixel would be 1/300th of an inch square – giving a much finer, less blocky result.

When working on images that will eventually be printed on a printing press, you need to work on high-resolution images. These are images whose resolution is twice the halftone screen frequency (measured in lines per inch – lpi) that will be used for final output – that is when you output to film, or directly to plate.

For example, for a final output screen frequency of 150 lpi – a typical screen frequency used for glossy magazines – you need to capture your image at a resolution of 300 ppi.

Resolutions of double the screen frequency are important for images with fine lines, repeating patterns or textures. You can achieve acceptable results, especially when printing at screen frequencies greater than 133 lpi, using resolutions of 1½ times the final screen frequency.

To work with images for positional purposes only, as long as you can get accurate enough on-screen results and laser proofs, you can work with much lower resolutions.

Hot tip

Images intended for multimedia presentations or the World Wide Web need only be 72 ppi, which is effectively the screen resolution.

RGB and CMYK Color Models

You need to be aware of two color models as you start working with Adobe Photoshop. These are the RGB (Red, Green, Blue) and CMYK (Cyan, Magenta, Yellow and blacK) color models.

RGB is important because it mirrors the way the human eye perceives color. It is the model used by scanners and digital cameras to capture color information in digital format, and it is the way that your computer monitor describes color.

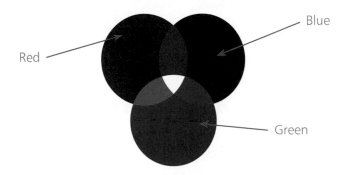

Red, green and blue are referred to as the "additive primaries". You can add varying proportions of the three colors to produce millions of different colors – but still a more limited range (or "gamut") than in nature, due to the limitations of the monitor. If you add 100% red, green and blue light together, you get white. You produce the "secondary" colors when you add red and blue to get magenta; green and blue to get cyan; red and green to get yellow.

The CMYK color model is referred to as the "subtractive" color model. It is important because this is the color model used by printing presses. If you subtract all cyan, magenta and yellow when printing you end up with the complete absence of color – white.

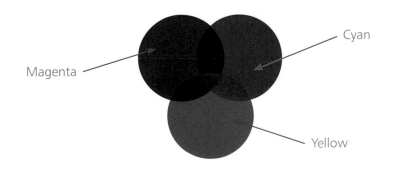

Hot tip

On the printing press, cyan, magenta, yellow and black combine to simulate a huge variety of colors. Printers add black because, although in theory, if you combine 100% each of cyan, magenta and yellow you produce black, in reality, because of impurities in the dyes, you only get a muddy brown.

Color gamuts

Color gamut refers to the range of colors that a specific device is capable of producing. There are millions of colors in the visible spectrum that the eye can discern. Scanners, monitors and printing presses cannot reproduce every color in the visible spectrum – the range of colors they are capable of producing is their gamut.

From the desktop publishing point of view, the process of capturing digital color information, viewing and manipulating this on-screen and then finally printing the image using colored inks is complicated, because the gamut of a color monitor is different to the gamut of CMYK and PANTONE inks. There are colors (especially vibrant yellows and deep blues) that can be displayed on a monitor but cannot be printed using traditional CMYK inks.

Typically you will work in RGB mode if the image is intended for use on the World Wide Web or in a multimedia presentation. You can work in CMYK or RGB mode if the image is intended for print, but you must remember to convert to CMYK mode before saving/exporting in EPS or TIFF file format in order to use the image in a page layout application. Adobe InDesign can import CMYK or RGB images in native Photoshop (.PSD) file format.

Beware

When you convert from RGB to CMYK mode, Photoshop converts out-of-gamut colors (in this case, colors that can be seen on screen, but not printed) into their nearest printable equivalent.

Hot tip

The CIE (Commission Internationale de l'Eclairage) XYZ color model is a model that defines the visible spectrum which can be seen by a "standard" observer.
　Colors with the same lightness value fall within an approximately triangular flat plane (the Visible Spectrum area in the diagram opposite.) The x axis represents the amount of red in colors and the y axis indicates the amount of green. The z axis represents the lightness of colors.

CIE XYZ color model

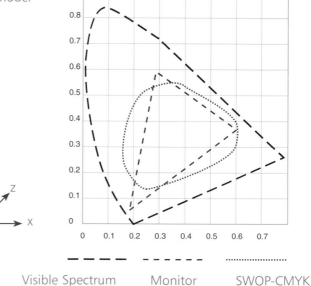

Visible Spectrum　　　Monitor　　　SWOP-CMYK

12

Color Management

No two devices that represent color, from digital camera to scanner to monitor to printer, will reproduce color in exactly the same way. The aim of a color management system is to ensure, as far as possible, that the colors you see on your screen are as close as possible to the colors you see in the finished work, whether in print or on screen.

Color management settings are available so that you can choose a color management workflow most suitable for your needs.

Using the Color Settings dialog box you can define how you manage color in your images as you work in Photoshop.

1 To specify color management settings for your Photoshop working environment, launch Photoshop, then choose Edit>Color Settings (Ctrl/Command+Shift+K).

2 Choose the most appropriate setting for your intended final output from the Settings pop-up list. For example, if you are using Photoshop for images that will be used in multimedia presentations, or on the World Wide Web, choose Web/Internet or Monitor Color options. If you are working with images that will be color separated then printed using CMYK inks, choose Europe or US Prepress defaults as appropriate.

Europe General Purpose 2	▼
Custom	
Other	
Europe General Purpose 2	
Europe Prepress 2	
Europe Web/Internet	
Monitor Color	

3 Only make changes to the default settings when you have gained experience of using Photoshop and you have a valid reason for making changes, or if you have consulted with your commercial printer and they have suggested changes to suit your specific output requirements.

Hot tip

If you use Photoshop with other applications in the Creative Suite, such as InDesign and Illustrator, it is recommended that you synchronize color settings across the suite using Adobe Bridge. In Bridge, choose Edit>Creative Suite Color Settings. Select a Color Settings option, then click Apply. (See pages 38–40 for information on Adobe Bridge.)

Hot tip

If you feel that you are not achieving good color in printed output, consult your commercial printer about creating custom settings for color management.

4 To get a better understanding of how the settings work in the Color Settings dialog box, roll your cursor over the pop-up lists. The Description area at the bottom of the palette updates with information on how the option affects the image.

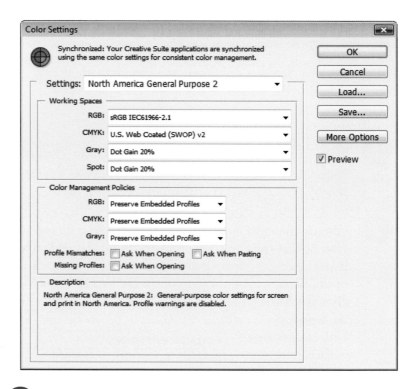

5 Click the More Options button to access advanced color management settings. Only change advanced settings if you have a detailed understanding of color management.

Hot tip

A CMS (Color Management System) is used to translate colors accurately from one color device to another. It attempts to represent a color consistently from the color space in which the image was created to the color space used at output, making adjustments so that color displays as consistently as possible across a range of monitors and other devices.

Monitor Calibration

Calibrate the monitor you are using in order to define the RGB color space that your monitor can display. Once you have calibrated your monitor, Photoshop can compensate for the differences between the color space in which your image resides and the color space of the monitor you are using.

Windows users can use the Adobe Gamma utility to calibrate the contrast and brightness, gamma (midtones), color balance and the white point of the monitor. Use the Adobe Gamma Wizard if you do not have previous experience of calibrating a monitor. For the Macintosh, use the Calibrate utility found in System Preferences>Displays.

Calibration settings that you create are saved as an ICC (International Color Consortium) profile with an .icm extension.

1. (Macintosh) Choose Apple Menu>System Preferences>Displays. Click the Color tab. Click the Calibrate button, then follow the on-screen prompts. (Windows) Choose Control Panel from the Start Menu. Double-click the Adobe Gamma icon to display the dialog box. Choose Step by Step (Wizard), then click the Next button.

2. Click the Load button to choose a monitor profile which matches the monitor you are using most closely. (Windows) Profiles are stored in the Windows\System32\spool\drivers\color folder. (Mac) Profiles are stored in the System/Library/ColorSync/Profiles folder.

15

Don't forget

It is important to calibrate your monitor so that colors in your image are displayed accurately. Calibrating your monitor should eliminate any color casts (typically reddish or blueish) on your monitor and ensure that the monitor displays grays as neutrally as possible.

Beware

Hardware-based color calibration utilities are more accurate than the Adobe Gamma utility. You should use only one calibration utility. Colors may appear incorrectly if you use more than one utility.

Hot tip

The easiest way to locate the Adobe Gamma utility in Windows Vista is to choose Start>Control Panel, then click the Classic View option in the sidebar on the left of the window.

...cont'd

Hot tip

Leave your monitor turned on for at least 30 minutes before you calibrate. This allows time for the display to warm up fully and stabilize.

Beware

For monitor calibration to be effective, you should not adjust the brightness and contrast settings on your monitor after you have completed the calibration process, and you must ensure that the lighting conditions within the room remain constant.

Don't forget

Recalibrate your monitor on a regular basis, as monitor performance can change over time.

3 Adjust the Brightness and Contrast settings of your monitor. Refer to the monitor handbook if you are unsure of how to adjust these settings. Click the Next button.

4 Only change the Phosphors pop-up if you know that your monitor's phosphors are different from the default selection. Click the Next button.

Phosphors: HDTV (CCIR 709)

5 With the View Single Gamma Only option selected, drag the Gamma slider until the square in the middle of the patterned lines fades, as far as possible, into

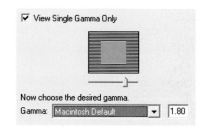

☑ View Single Gamma Only

Now choose the desired gamma.
Gamma: Macintosh Default | 1.80

the pattern. This defines the brightness of the midtones on your monitor. Click the Next button. For Desired Gamma choose a target gamma. For images intended for the World Wide Web or multimedia presentations, choose a gamma of 2.2. If you intend to print images using CMYK inks, you should typically choose a gamma of 1.8. Click the Next button.

6 Leave the Hardware White Point on the default setting unless you know this to be

Adjusted White Point: Same as Hardware

inaccurate. Click Next. Leave Adjusted White Point on Same as Hardware unless you want to view the image at a different color temperature to that set by the monitor's factory-specified setting. Click the Next button.

7 Click the Finish button to save settings as an .icm compatible profile. Name the profile and save it to the Color folder.

2 The Working Environment

This chapter covers the basics of the Photoshop working environment, getting you used to the Photoshop window, the Toolbox, palettes and a number of standard Photoshop conventions and techniques that you will find useful as you develop your Photoshop skills.

The Working Environment

There are four "screen modes" to choose from when working on images in Photoshop. The screen mode icons are located at the bottom of the Toolbox.

■	Standard Screen Mode	F
	Maximized Screen Mode	F
	Full Screen Mode With Menu Bar	F
	Full Screen Mode	F

Standard Screen mode

Maximized Screen mode displays a maximized image window which automatically resizes to accommodate the Palette dock as you expand/collapse it. Full Screen with Menu Bar mode is useful when working on individual images because it clears away the clutter of the Finder environment (Mac), or the Windows desktop. Use Full Screen mode to see the image without the distraction of other screen elements, and without any other colors interfering with the colors in your image.

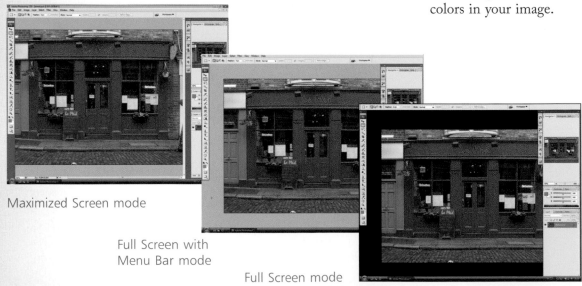

Maximized Screen mode

Full Screen with Menu Bar mode

Full Screen mode

Windows environment

The Windows environment offers identical functionality to the Macintosh environment, as you can see from a comparison of the Windows and Macintosh application window screen shots.

The Image window

Close button — Title bar

— Image

— Scroll bars

View % — Resize box

Don't forget

Command (often referred to as "Apple" on the Mac) and Ctrl (Windows), and Alt/ option (Mac) and Alt (Windows) are used identically as modifier keys. Shift is standard on both platforms. This book uses Alt, with an uppercase "A" to denote both the Macintosh and Windows key of that name.

Don't forget

Windows users can use the right mouse button to access context sensitive menus; Mac users can hold down the Control key and press their single mouse button.

Hot tip

Every time you launch Photoshop the Welcome screen appears. Click on one of the listed links, or click the Close button to start working with Photoshop. To prevent the Welcome screen appearing the next time you launch Photoshop, deselect the Show this dialog at startup option.

Using the Toolbox

There are a number of useful general techniques that relate to choosing tools in the Toolbox, including those from the expanded range of hidden tool pop-ups.

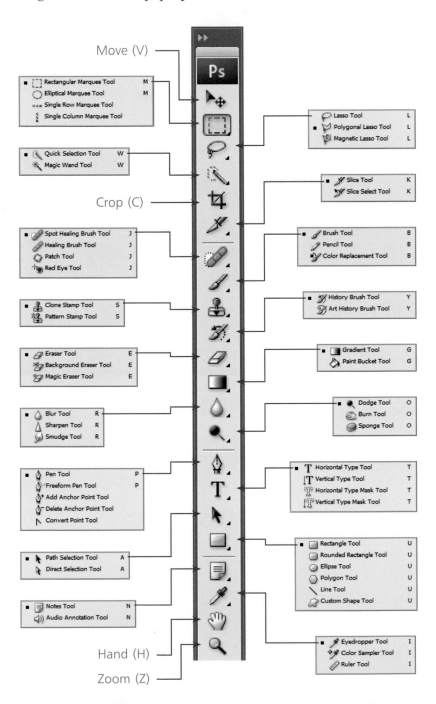

...cont'd

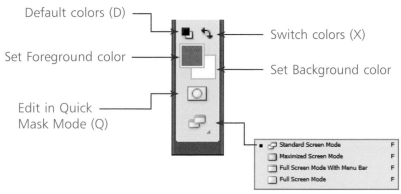

Default colors (D)

Switch colors (X)

Set Foreground color

Set Background color

Edit in Quick
Mask Mode (Q)

	Standard Screen Mode	F
	Maximized Screen Mode	F
	Full Screen Mode With Menu Bar	F
	Full Screen Mode	F

Toolbox techniques

1 Press the keyboard shortcut listed in the tool pop-up to access tools.

2 Click and hold on any tool with a small triangle in the bottom right corner to see all tools in that tool group.

3 Hold down Alt/option and click on any tool in a tool group to cycle through the available tools. Alternatively, hold down Shift, then press the keyboard shortcut for that tool group a number of times. For example, press "O" three times to cycle through all the tools in the Dodge tool group.

4 Press Tab to hide/show all palettes, including the toolbox. Hold down Shift, then press the Tab key to hide/show all palettes except the Toolbox.

5 Press Caps Lock to change the painting or brush size cursor to a precise crosshair cursor, which indicates the center of the painting tool. Press Caps Lock again to return to the standard cursor display.

6 When you select a tool in the Toolbox, the Options bar, extending across the top of the Photoshop window, updates according to the tool you select. Get into the habit of checking the settings in the Options bar before you proceed to use the tool.

Hot tip

Choose Edit>
Preferences>Cursors
(Windows), or
Photoshop>Preferences>
Cursors (Mac) to change
the default appearance
of painting and other
cursors.

Document and Scratch Sizes

The Sizes bar is useful for monitoring disk space and memory considerations as you work on your images.

Document Sizes

With Document Sizes selected, you see two numbers separated by a slash. The first number is

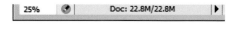

the size of the image with all layers flattened. The second number may be larger and represents the file storage size whilst the image contains additional layers and/or alpha channels you may have set up. In images that consist of only a single layer, with no additional channels, both numbers are the same.

Scratch Sizes

The Scratch disk is an underlying technical detail that you should be aware of when using Photoshop. The Scratch disk is a designated hard disk that Photoshop uses as "virtual" memory if it runs out of memory (RAM) whilst working on one or more images.

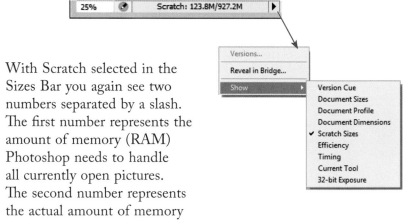

With Scratch selected in the Sizes Bar you again see two numbers separated by a slash. The first number represents the amount of memory (RAM) Photoshop needs to handle all currently open pictures. The second number represents the actual amount of memory available to Photoshop. When the first number is greater than the second, Photoshop is using the Scratch disk as virtual memory.

As a general rule of thumb when working in Photoshop, you should have free disk space of at least 3-5 times the file size of the image you are working on. This is because Photoshop makes use of the Scratch disk as virtual memory and because Photoshop needs to hold more than one copy of the image you are working on for the Undo, Revert and History palette functions.

Ruler Guides and Grids

You can show a grid in your image window to help with alignment and measuring, and you can also drag in ruler guides. Both sets of guides are non-printing. Customize the appearance of the grid and guides using Edit>Preferences>Guides, Grid & Slices (Windows), Photoshop>Preferences>Guides, Grid & Slices (Mac).

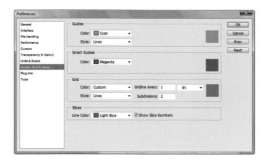

Hot tip

Make sure you select View>Snap To>Guides/ Grid, if you want cursors and selections to snap to guides and the grid. These options are very useful for aligning elements accurately.

1. To show or hide the grid, choose View>Show/Hide Grid.

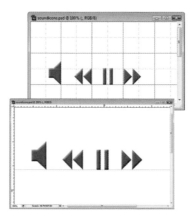

2. To create a ruler guide, first choose View>Rulers to display the rulers along the top and left edges of the image window. Position your cursor in a ruler and then click and drag onto your image to create either a vertical or horizontal guide.

Hot tip

Use keyboard shortcuts: Ctrl/Command+; to Hide/Show ruler guides; Ctrl/Command+' to Hide/Show the grid.

3. To reposition a ruler guide, select the Move tool, position your cursor on a guide, then click and drag. The cursor changes to a bi-directional arrow when you pick up a guide. To remove a ruler guide, drag the ruler guide back into the ruler it came from. Alternatively, choose View>Clear Guides to remove all guides.

Beware

Take care when repositioning ruler guides that you don't reposition an entire layer accidentally. Make sure you see the bi-directional arrows which indicate that you are dragging a guide.

4. To temporarily hide any grid or guides in order to preview the image without the clutter of non-printing guides, choose View>Extras (Ctrl/Command+H). Use the same command to bring back the guides and grid.

Moving Around

Use any combination of the Navigator palette, the Zoom tool, the Hand tool and the scroll bars for moving around and zooming in and out of your image.

1 Choose Window>Show Navigator, or click the Navigator dock icon to show the Navigator palette if it is not already visible in the Palette dock. In the palette, you can double-click the % entry box, enter a zoom % (0.15 – 3200%), then press Return/Enter.

Alternatively, drag the zoom slider to the right to zoom in, or to the left to zoom out. Each time you change your zoom level, the view in the Preview area updates.

2 Drag the red View box in the Preview area to move quickly to different areas of your image.

3 To use the Zoom tool, select it, position your cursor on the image and click to zoom in on the area around your cursor, in preset increments. With the Zoom tool selected, hold down Alt/option. The cursor changes to the zoom out cursor; click to zoom out in the preset increments.

4 With the Zoom tool selected, you can also click and drag to define the area you want to zoom in on.

5 You can use the Hand tool in addition to using the scroll bars to move around your image when you have zoomed in on it. Select the tool, position your cursor on the image, then click and drag to reposition.

Hot tip

Hold down Ctrl/Command and the Spacebar to temporarily access the Zoom tool with any other tool selected. Add the Alt/option key to the above combination to zoom out.

Hot tip

With any other tool selected, hold down the Spacebar to temporarily access the Hand tool.

The Info Palette

The Info palette (Window>Info) provides useful numerical read-outs relative to the position of the cursor on your image.

You can use it as an on-screen densitometer to examine color values at the cursor. There are two color read-outs. As a default, the first color read-out is the actual color under the cursor. For example, a read-out of red, green, and blue color components in an RGB image. The default second read-out is for cyan, magenta, yellow and black values.

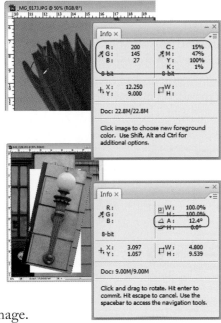

The palette also displays x and y coordinates, giving the precise location of the cursor as it moves over the image.

If you create a selection, there is a read-out of the width and height of the selection. The palette also displays values for some options such as rotating, skewing and scaling selections.

25

Beware

An exclamation mark next to the CMYK readouts indicates that a color is outside the printable CMYK gamut or range of colors:

1. To change the default settings for the Info Palette, choose Palette Options from the Info palette menu ( ).

2. Use the Mode pop-ups to choose the first and second color read-outs.

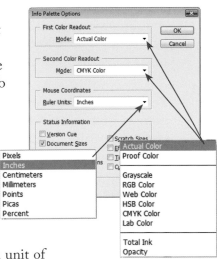

3. You can also choose a unit of measurement for mouse coordinates.

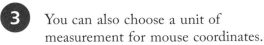

Palette Techniques

The default palette dock on the right of the Photoshop window contains 17 palettes in two columns. You can expand or collapse the display of each palette dock and you can rearrange palettes to suit your individual working preferences. In its default arrangement, the main dock is expanded and the secondary dock is collapsed.

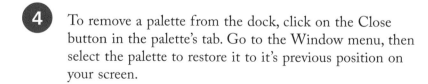

Hot tip

Choose Window>
Workspace>Default
Workspace to recreate
Photoshop's default
arrangement of the
palette dock.

Hot tip

Drag the Resize icon
( ) in the bottom right
corner of a palette to
increase/decrease its size.

1 To expand a palette dock, click the Expand Dock button ( ) in the top right corner of the dock. Click the Collapse to Icons button ( ) to shrink the display of palettes to icons.

2 To manually resize the width of the docks, drag the resize bars ( ).

3 Click on a palette tab to make the palette active so that it's controls become available. An active palette displays a Close button next to it's name.

4 To remove a palette from the dock, click on the Close button in the palette's tab. Go to the Window menu, then select the palette to restore it to it's previous position on your screen.

Palette Groups

The palettes in the palette dock are arranged in groups initially. For example, Layers, Channels and Paths form a group. There are a number of techniques you can use to control the appearance of palette groups.

Don't forget

The Options palette runs
along the top of the
Photoshop application
window. The Animation
palette is not included in
the default palette dock.
Both can be accessed
from the Window menu.

1 To hide all palettes in a palette group, click the group's Close button (⊠). If you hide a complete group, selecting any of the palettes from the Window menu redisplays the full palette group.

2 To collapse the appearance to tabs only, click the Maximize/Minimize icon in the top right of the palette group bar, or click anywhere in the gray title bar area of the palette.

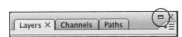

Floating and combining palettes
To provide complete flexibility in the way you manage palettes, each palette can be made into a floating palette, or you can combine palettes into your own custom groupings.

1 To create a floating palette, position your cursor on the palettes's tab, then drag the palette out from the group – typically into the image window. To reposition the floating palette, drag it's tab or the palette's gray title bar.

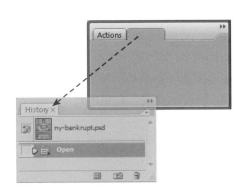

2 To combine a palette with another palette group, drag the palette's tab or gray title bar into the palette group. Release the mouse when the palette group highlights in blue.

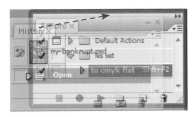

Hot tip

All palettes have a palette menu for accessing a range of commands or options relevant to the palette. Click the palette menu button ( ) to access the palette menu.

Hot tip

Press the Tab key to hide/show all palettes including the Toolbox. Hold down Shift, then press Tab to hide/show currently visible palettes, with the exception of the Toolbox.

Hot tip

Choose Window> Workspace>Save Workspace to save the current position of your palettes. Enter a name for this workspace arrangement in the Save Workspace dialog box. Choose Window>Workspace then select the name of the workspace to reset palettes to this arrangement.

27

Save and Load Custom Settings

The Swatches, Styles and Actions palettes, the Brushes presets, along with dialog boxes such as Duotones, Levels and Curves, have Save and Load options which allow you to save custom settings made in the palette or dialog box and then load them into the same image, or into other Photoshop images, when required. The following example uses the Swatches palette.

1 After creating a custom Swatches palette (see Chapter 4), choose Save Swatches in the palette menu (in a dialog box, click the Save button).

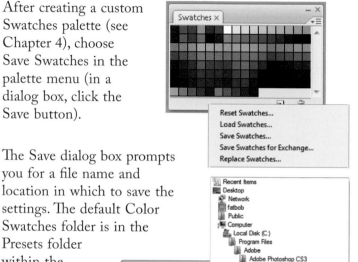

2 The Save dialog box prompts you for a file name and location in which to save the settings. The default Color Swatches folder is in the Presets folder within the Photoshop CS3 folder. The extension for a Color Swatches file is .ACO. Make sure you save the file with the correct extension.

3 To load previously saved settings, choose Replace Swatches or Load Swatches in the palette menu (in a dialog box click the Load button), then specify the location of the settings you previously saved. Click on the settings file name, then click Open. Load Swatches adds the new swatches to the existing swatches in the palette. Replace Swatches replaces the current swatches with the new set.

Hot tip

When you save settings, you create an independent settings file which stores the custom information. You can load these settings into other images as necessary.

Hot tip

In the Brushes palette, select a brush set from the bottom of the Brushes palette menu. Try Assorted Brushes as a starting point for experimenting with different brush types.

Hot tip

Choose Reset Swatches in the palette menu to restore settings to their original defaults.

Printing

When you have made all the necessary edits and adjustments to an image you are ready to print. The Print dialog box has a color managed thumbnail preview of the image and you can access additional print features and a preview of the image as it will print on the specified paper size.

1 Choose File>Print. Make sure the correct printer is selected from the Printer pop-up menu. Enter the number of copies you want to print. Some options are available only if you are printing to a PostScript printer.

2 Click the Page Setup button to set controls specific to your printer. In particular, make sure the Paper Type and Size are set correctly, check that the orientation is appropriate and select a quality option. Refer to the manufacturer's manual for information on the options available for the printer. Click OK.

3 If necessary, click the Scale to Fit Media checkbox to reduce the size of the image so that it fits onto the specified paper size.

4 OK the Print dialog box to print a copy of the image. Click Done if you want to save changes in the dialog box and return to the image without printing it.

Beware

The exact appearance of the Page Setup dialog box varies according to the printer selected.

Hot tip

In the Print dialog box, click the Color Management option, then choose Output from the drop down menu to specify additional printed information such as Crop Marks and Calibration bars. As you switch on the various options they appear in the preview area.

Beware

In the Print dialog box, only change Color Management options if you are not satisfied with your printed output. In some cases, choosing Let Photoshop Determine Colors from the Color Management pop-up can produce improved color output.

Picture Package

The Picture Package command enables you to print multiple copies of an image, at various sizes, on a single sheet of paper.

1 To create a Picture Package, choose File>Automate>Picture Package. Select the image you want to use from the Use pop-up menu.

2 From the Document area, choose the page size you want to print onto. Then choose a layout arrangement from the Layout pop-up. The Layout area on the right updates to indicate the positioning of the images. Specify Resolution and Color Mode options.

3 Use the Content pop-up to choose a label type if required. Select Custom Text to enter details in the Custom Text field. Control the appearance and position of text labels using the other controls.

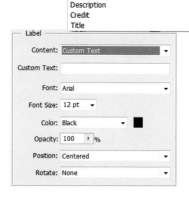

4 When you OK the dialog box, Photoshop prepares the multiple copies of the image as a single picture package file which you can print or save.

The History Palette

Every time you modify an image Photoshop records this as a new state in the History palette. The palette records the last 20 states of the image. Use the History palette to return to a previous state of the image within the current work session. The most recent state of the image appears at the bottom of the list in the palette.

1 To return to a previous state of the image, click on a state in the History palette. The image reverts to that stage of the work session. States after the state you click on are dimmed. These subsequent states are discarded if you continue to work from the selected state.

2 Alternatively, drag the state slider up or down to indicate the state you wish to move to. Or, choose Step Forward/Step Backward from the palette menu ( ), to move sequentially through the states.

Deleting states

Delete states from the History palette to remove the changes to the image recorded by that state and all subsequent states.

1 To delete a history state, click on its name, then choose Delete from the palette menu. Alternatively, drag the state into the Wastebasket icon at the bottom of the palette.

Step Forward	Shift+Ctrl+Z
Step Backward	Alt+Ctrl+Z
New Snapshot...	
Delete	
Clear History	
New Document	
History Options...	

Clearing states

Clearing states leaves the image at its current state, but removes all previous states from the History palette.

1 To clear the History palette, use the palette menu to choose Clear History. All recorded states are deleted from the History palette, leaving the image at its most recent state.

Hot tip

You can also use the keyboard shortcuts Ctrl/Command+Shift+Z to move to the next state. Use Ctrl/Command+Alt/option+Z to move to the previous state.

Beware

Both techniques for deleting states delete the selected state and all states that occur after it. In other words, you are reverting to the state of the image previous to the state you delete.

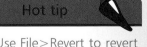

Hot tip

Use File>Revert to revert to the state of your image as it was when you last did a File>Save. The Revert command appears as a state in the History palette.

...cont'd

Purging states

Purging states is useful if you get a low memory message. This is typically because the Undo buffer is becoming full with the changes to the image that it is having to record. When you purge states they are deleted from the Undo buffer, freeing up memory.

1 To purge states, hold down Alt/option, then choose Clear History from the palette menu in the History palette. This command purges history states from the active image. Choose Edit>Purge>Histories if you want to purge all history states for all open images.

Snapshots

An initial "snapshot" is created by default when you open an image. This appears at the top of the History palette. As you work on the image, the History palette records the results of the last 20 operations performed. Older states of the image are automatically deleted to keep memory free for Photoshop. You can keep particular states of an image during a work session by making additional snapshots.

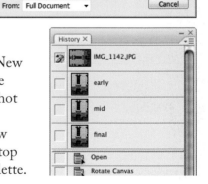

1 To create additional snapshots, click on any state in the History palette. Choose New Snapshot from the palette menu. In the New Snapshot dialog box enter a name. OK the dialog box. A new snapshot is added in the top section of the History palette.

2 Click on a snapshot to revert to the state of the image when the snapshot was created. If you then continue to work on the image, all history states are lost.

3 To delete a snapshot, click once on the snapshot to select it, then click on the Wastebasket icon at the bottom of the palette.

3 Open and Save Files

Opening and converting files to a wide range of formats to suit varied output requirements is one of Photoshop's great strengths.

This chapter covers a range of essential techniques for opening and saving images in Photoshop.

Opening Images in Photoshop

After you launch Photoshop you can open images using the File menu. The Adobe Bridge provides a powerful and flexible alternative method for locating and opening images (see page 38 for further information).

(see page 38 for further information)

Hot tip

Double-click Photoshop file icons in the Windows or Macintosh file-management environments to open the file. If Photoshop is not running, this also launches Photoshop.

1 To open an image from within Photoshop, choose File>Open. This takes you into the Open dialog box. Navigate through folders and sub-folders as necessary to locate the file you wish to open, click on the file name to select it, then click Open. Alternatively, just double-click the file name.

2 Select the Show All Readable Documents (Mac), or choose All Formats from the Files of type pop-up (Windows), to show all files in the selected folder.

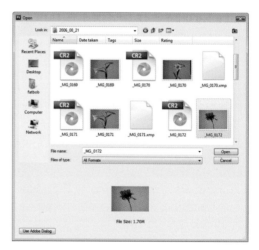

3 You can also open recently opened files by choosing File>Open Recent. Select a file from the list.

Hot tip

Choose Edit> Preferences>File Handling (Windows), or, Photoshop Preferences>File Handling (Mac), then enter a number for Recent file list contains to control the number of files that appear in the Recent files sub-menu.

4 (Mac) To search for a file that you want to open from within the Open dialog box, click the Find button. Enter the file name, then click Find/Find Again, until you find the file.

Scanning into Photoshop

You can scan into Photoshop using the File>Import sub menu. Make sure you install the scanning software for your scanner before you begin.

1 To create a scan from within Photoshop, choose File>Import, then select the appropriate scanner from the sub-menu.

Typically, you can either scan using the scanner's default settings, or you can customize settings including: scan mode (grayscale, color, line art etc.), resolution, scale, contrast, brightness and gamma. Refer to your scanning software manual for details of the controls available.

Many of the scanning controls have equivalent functions in Photoshop. Scanning options vary from scanner to scanner, but you should be able to specify whether you are scanning a transparency or a photograph. The other essential decisions you need to make at this stage are image mode, resolution and scale. You may also need to specify a crop area in the preview window.

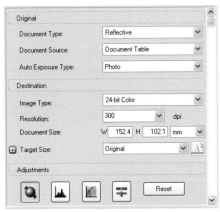

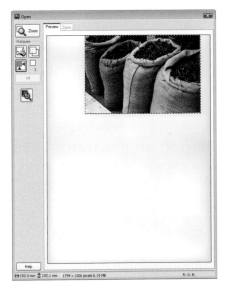

2 Click the Scan button. Wait until the scanning process finishes and the image appears in an untitled Photoshop window. Save the image.

Hot tip

For WIA compliant scanners, choose File>Import>WIA Support. In the WIA Support dialog box click the Browse button to specify a location in which to save the scanned image, then click the Start button. Select your scanner in the Select Device dialog box. Click OK to begin the scan. Select scanner specific options as necessary. Refer to the manufacturer's manual for detailed information on the options available.

Opening and Placing EPS files

EPS stands for Encapsulated Postscript. EPS files can contain bitmap as well as vector information. EPS files, created in applications such as Adobe Illustrator, typically contain object-oriented or "vector" format information.

Opening an Illustrator EPS file

When you open an EPS file in Photoshop, it is rasterized: the vector information is converted into Photoshop's pixel-based format.

1 To open an EPS file as a new document, choose File>Open. Locate and highlight the EPS file you want to open, then click the Open button. Alternatively, double-click the file name.

2 In the Rasterize dialog box, enter new dimensions for Width and Height if required. Enter the resolution required for your final output device and choose an image mode from the Mode pop-up menu.

3 Select the Constrain Proportions box to keep the original proportions of the EPS. Select Anti-aliased to slightly blur pixels along edges to avoid unwanted jagged edges. Click OK. The EPS appears in its own image window. It is now a bitmap image.

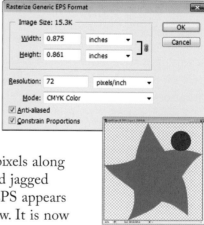

Placing an Illustrator EPS file

You can also "place" an Illustrator EPS file into an open Photoshop document. The placed artwork appears on a new Smart Objects layer.

1 To place an EPS file into an existing Photoshop file, first open an image in Photoshop, or create a new document.

Hot tip

Before you accept the placed EPS, you can also use the Options bar to change position, size, rotation and skew values numerically for the file.

2 Choose File>Place. Use the Place dialog box to specify the location and name of the EPS file, then click the Place button.

Beware

To create anti-aliased edges for a placed EPS, you must select the Anti-aliased option in the Options bar before you click the Accept button.

3 A bounding box with eight "handles" and a cross through the placed image appears in the Photoshop image window. The EPS image itself may take a few seconds to draw inside the bounding box.

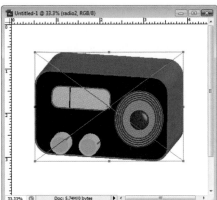

Hot tip

If you don't want to accept the placed image, with the bounding box still visible press the Esc key. If you have already placed the image you can delete the new layer. (See page 114.)

4 If necessary, drag a corner handle to resize the placed image. Hold down Shift as you drag to maintain proportions. Position your cursor inside the bounding box of the placed image and drag to reposition the image.

Hot tip

You can copy vector artwork from Illustrator into Photoshop using the clipboard. In Illustrator, copy selected artwork using Edit>Copy, then, in Photoshop, choose Edit>Paste. Choose Path in the Paste dialog box to import the artwork as paths in the Paths palette:

5 When you are satisfied, click the Commit button in the Options bar, press Return/Enter, or double-click inside the bounding box. The rasterized file is placed on a new Smart Objects layer.

Bridge

Adobe Bridge provides a powerful, visual environment for locating, organizing and tracking image files and other digital assets on your system. Click the Go to Bridge button in the Options bar to launch Bridge from within Photoshop.

Hot tip

You can launch Bridge as a standalone application, as you would launch any other application – from the Start>Programs menu in Windows, or from the Applications folder on the Mac.

Favorites view

Favorites view gives you access to a variety of Adobe services such as Adobe Stock Photos and Adobe Photographers Directory. You need an internet connection to access these services. For quick access to image folders you use frequently you can create your own favorites folders.

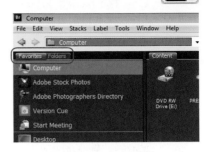

1 To create a new favorites folder, click the Favorites tab, then click the Computer icon. Navigate to the folder in the Contents pane. Click once on the folder to select it, then drag it into the Favorites pane below the divider bar.

Hot tip

You can create a Favorites folder from the Folders tab. Navigate to a specific folder, position your cursor on the folder then right-click (Windows) or Ctrl+click (Mac). Select Add to Favorites from the context menu.

2 To remove a folder from the Favorites pane, position your cursor on the folder then right-click (Windows) or Ctrl+click (Mac). Select Remove from Favorites from the context menu.

Folders view

Click the Folders tab to view, manage, sort and open images on your system. You can also use the Folder view to create new folders and to rename, move, delete and rank image files.

Hot tip

To move a file, position your cursor on the image thumbnail, then drag it to a different folder in the Folder panel of the Bridge window. To copy a file to a new location, hold down Alt/option, then drag it to a different folder.

1 In the Bridge window, click the Folder tab. Use the Folder pane to navigate to specific folders on your hard disk using standard Windows/Macintosh techniques.

...cont'd

2 The Content pane in the middle column of the window displays thumbnail previews of the contents of the selected folder. When you click on a thumbnail in the Content pane a larger version of the image appears in the Preview pane.

3 You can set up to 3 preferred workspace views using the numbered View buttons. (See Hot Tip opposite.) Click once on a View button to change the arrangement of the Bridge window.

4 File information for a selected image file appears in the Metadata and Keyword panes. With the Metadata tab selected, click the expand triangle to the left of Camera Data (EXIF) to view image information imported from a digital camera. You can also use options from the palette menu for each tab to add and edit metadata and keyword information for your image files. Use the Expand/Collapse triangle to display/hide information for each category.

Hot tip

Drag the Thumbnail Size slider, at the bottom of the window, to control the size of thumbnail previews in the contents area.

Hot tip

To associate a workspace view to a numbered view button ( ), position your cursor on the button, then press the button and hold it down briefly to access the Workspace views pop-up menu. Select a preset view to associate it with the View button:

Hot tip

Choose an option from the View>Sort sub-menu to control the way image thumbnails are ordered in the Preview pane.

...cont'd

5 Use the Metadata palette menu button (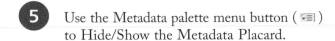) to Hide/Show the Metadata Placard.

6 To open a file from the Content area, click on an image thumbnail to select it, then press the Enter/Return key. You can also double-click a thumbnail. If you open a Camera Raw image it opens in the Camera Raw dialog box. (See pages 42–43 for information on Camera Raw.)

7 To create a 1–5 star ranking for an image, click a dot below the thumbnail to convert it to a star. To remove stars, click the star to the left of the star you want to remove, or click to the left of all stars to remove the ranking. Alternatively, use the Label menu to apply star ratings to a selected image.

8 Use the Filter pane to display only thumbnails with a specific rating. If necessary, click the Ratings expand triangle, then click to the left of the star ratings to display images with a particular rating.

Working with stacks

You can create "stacks" of multiple variations of the same image to use space in the Contents area more effectively. A stack brings thumbnails together as a group that can be expanded or collapsed.

1 Select the multiple images you want to include in the stack. Use the Ctrl/Command key to select more than one image at the same time.

...cont'd

2   Choose Stack>Group as Stack. The selected images appear as overlapping image thumbnails stacked one on top of another. A stack number icon appears in the top left corner to indicate the number of images in the stack.

Group as Stack	Ctrl+G
Ungroup from Stack	Ctrl+Shft+G
Close Stack	Ctrl+Left Arrow
Promote to Top of Stack	
Expand All Stacks	Ctrl+Alt+Right Arrow
Collapse All Stacks	Ctrl+Alt+Left Arrow
Frame Rate	▸

Hot tip

Choose Window>
Workspace>Vertical
Filmstrip, (which provides
a large preview area),
then select two or more
thumbnails to compare
them in the Preview area.

3   Click the stack number icon, or choose Stack>Open Stack to reveal all image thumbnails in the stack. To compress the stack click the stack number icon again, or choose Stack>Close Stack.

Hot tip

Choose File>Get
Photos from Camera to
download images from
a connected camera
onto your computer and
directly into Bridge.

4   To release all images from a stack, make sure the stack is closed, then choose Stack>Ungroup from Stack. To remove an individual image from a stack, select the image in an open stack, then choose Stack>Ungroup from Stack.

Using the Loupe

The "Loupe", a small magnifying glass window, provides a magnified preview of areas in an image so that you can check fine detail.

1   To access the Loupe, position your cursor in the preview image. Click when the cursor changes to the Zoom icon. To reposition the Loupe over different parts of the preview image position your cursor on the pointed, top left corner of the Loupe, then drag. To cancel the Loupe click anywhere inside the Loupe display.

Hot tip

Use the "+" (plus)
and "-" (minus) keys to
zoom the Loupe display
in or out.

Adobe Camera Raw

When you capture a raw image, the camera does not process the color data in the image, apply compression settings such as JPEG, make tonal adjustments nor set white balance and other values. Using the Camera Raw dialog box gives you precise control over how you manipulate the raw digital color information captured by the camera.

1 To open a camera raw image, launch Bridge. (See pages 38–41 for information on using Bridge.) Double-click a camera raw image in Bridge to open the image in the Camera Raw window.

2 From Photoshop, choose File>Open. Browse to a Camera Raw file, select it, then click the Open button.

The Camera Raw window contains an extensive range of commands for manipulating the raw image data captured by the camera.

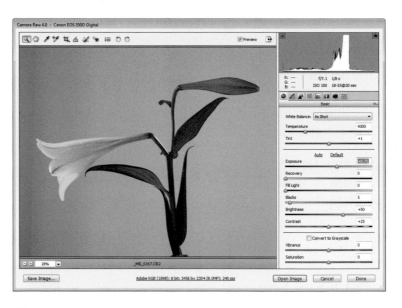

1 The Histogram in the top right corner of the window provides visual feedback in real time on changes you make to settings in the tabbed control panels area of the window. When you first start to work with Camera Raw images, begin by using the Basic tab (🔘) controls to adjust white balance, tone and saturation. More advanced controls provided in the remaining tabs allow you to fine tune your initial settings. (See Hot Tip opposite.)

2 The Histogram info area provides useful information about the camera and some of the exposure settings used to capture the image.

3 The Tool Bar, running along the top of the window provides basic tools for zooming, panning, setting White Balance, color sample points, cropping, straightening and rotating which, with the exception of White Balance, are similar to controls available within Photoshop. There is also a Red Eye removal tool and a Retouch tool.

4 Use the Zoom controls in the bottom left of the window to zoom in or out on the image. You can also use any other standard Photoshop magnification techniques.

5 Workflow Options along the bottom of the window provide useful information on color space, file size, bit depth and resolution. To change any of these settings, click the workflow link to display the Workflow Options dialog box.

Saving Camera Raw Images

1 When you are satisfied with your settings you can click the Open Image button to open a copy of the Camera Raw file in Photoshop if you want to do further work on it.

2 Click the Save Image button to save a copy of the Camera Raw file in JPEG, PSD, TIFF or DNG format.

3 Click the Done button to save the current settings with the original Camera Raw file and close the Camera Raw dialog box.

Hot tip

The tabbed controls available in the Camera Raw dialog box are:
- Basic,
- Tone Curve,
- Detail,
- HSL/Grayscale,
- Split Toning,
- Lens Correction,
- Camera Calibration,
- Presets.

Hot tip

A processed image icon (▤) appears in Bridge thumbnails after you edit settings for a camera raw file.

Hot tip

DNG – Digital Negative file format is a non-proprietary format, developed by Adobe, which should ensure that images archived in this format remain easily accessible in the future.

Saving Files

The basic principles of saving files in Photoshop – using "Save" and "Save As" – are the same as in any other Macintosh or Windows application. Save regularly as you modify an image so that you do not lose any changes you make should a system crash occur. You should use Save As to save a new file in the first instance, to make copies of a file, to save a file to a new location and when you need to save an image in a different file format.

Photoshop supports numerous file formats for opening and saving images. Typically, you save an image in a particular format to meet specific output or printing specifications, to compress the image to save disk space, or to open or import the image into an application that requires a particular file format.

1 To save an image in the first instance, choose File>Save As. Specify where you want to save the file. Enter a name for the file. Use the Format pop-up to choose an appropriate format. Click the Save button. File extensions are added automatically.

2 To save changes as you work on an image, choose File>Save. The previously saved file information is updated.

Photoshop format

Use this format as you work on your image – all Photoshop options, in particular layers, remain available to you in this format. Photoshop also performs open and save routines more quickly when using its native format.

TIFF Format

TIFF (Tagged Image File Format) became a standard file format for scanned images in the early days of desktop publishing. It is common on both Mac and Windows platforms and is compatible with most paint, image-editing and page layout applications.

1 To save an image in TIFF format, choose File>Save As. The Save As dialog box appears. Specify where you want to save the image and enter a name in the name entry box. Use the Format pop-up menu to choose TIFF, then click OK.

File name:	goldman3x3.tif
Format:	TIFF (*.TIF;*.TIFF)

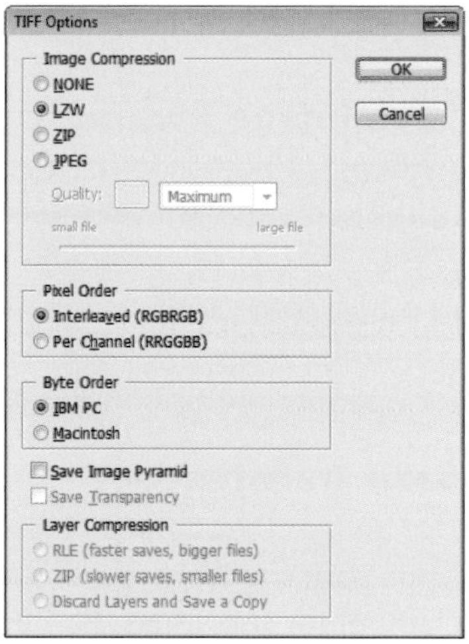

2 The TIFF Options dialog box appears. Select Image Compression and other options as required, then OK the dialog box.

Pixel Order
Early versions of Photoshop wrote tiffs with channel order interleaved. Per Channel usually produces better compression. Both are compatible with earlier versions of Photoshop.

Byte Order
Use this option to specify whether you want the TIFF to be used on a Mac or a PC, as Mac and PC TIFF formats vary slightly. Most recently released applications can read files using either option.

LZW Compression
(Lempel-Zif-Welch) is a compression format that looks for repeated elements in the computer code that describes the image and replaces these with shorter sequences. It is a "lossless"

Hot tip

On the Macintosh, choose Photoshop>Preferences>File Handling to specify whether or not you want file extensions – e.g. ".tif" – automatically added when saving files.

Hot tip

A warning appears at the bottom of the Save As dialog box if an image uses features, such as layers or alpha channels, that are not supported by that particular file format. You are prompted to save a copy of the file. Photoshop automatically adds the word "copy" to the file name.

...cont'd

Hot tip

4 gigabytes is the maximum file size for tiff images in Photoshop.

compression scheme – none of the image's detail is lost. Applications such as QuarkXPress and Adobe InDesign can import TIFFs with LZW compression.

Zip
Zip is a lossless compression format and achieves greatest compression in images that contain areas of solid color. Zip compression is supported by PDF and TIFF file formats.

JPEG
JPEG is a "lossy" compression format (see page 211). JPEG compression is most suitable for photographic type images with variations in highlight and shadow detail throughout the image. (See page 211 for further information on choosing quality options for JPEG compression.)

Save Image Pyramid
Although Photoshop itself cannot work with multiple resolutions in the same file, you can select the Save Image Pyramid option to preserve multiple resolutions already in a file. Some applications (such as Adobe InDesign) provide support for opening multiresolution files.

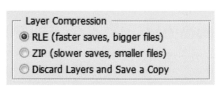

Save Transparency
For images that contain transparent areas you can select Save Transparency. Transparent areas are saved in an additional Alpha channel for use when the file is opened in a different application. Transparency is always retained when a file is opened in Photoshop.

Hot tip

You can save images in CMYK, RGB, Lab, Index Color and Grayscale using TIFF file format.

Layer Compression
Photoshop can read layer information saved in TIFF file format, although most other applications cannot. Files saved with layers are larger than image files that have been flattened into a single layer. Choose Layer Compression options to specify how pixel data in layers is compressed. RLE (Run Length Encoding) is a lossless compression format supported by many Windows file formats. Select Discard Layers and Save a Copy if you do not want to preserve layers in the image.

Photoshop EPS

EPS generates file sizes which can be two to four times greater than TIFFs with LZW compression. To save in EPS format, do the following:

 Follow the procedure for saving TIFFs, but choose Photoshop EPS from the Format pop-up menu. Click OK. The EPS Options dialog box appears. Specify your settings, then click OK.

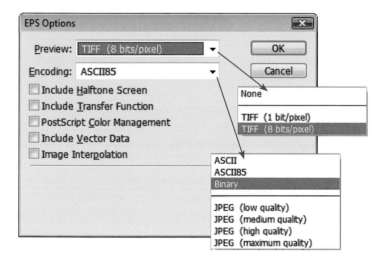

Preview

This option specifies the quality of the low-resolution screen preview you see when you import the image into applications such as Adobe InDesign and QuarkXPress. Use "Macintosh (8-bits/pixel)" for a color preview. "Macintosh (JPEG)" uses JPEG compression routines, but is only supported by PostScript Level 2 printers. Use TIFF if you want to use the image in Windows.

Encoding

The encoding option determines how image data is transmitted to the printing device. Use binary encoding if you want to export the image for use with Adobe Illustrator. Binary encoding typically produces a smaller file size. Some applications do not recognize binary encoding; in this case you have to use ASCII. JPEG encoding options discard image data in order to create smaller file sizes.

You can save Duotone, CMYK, RGB, Lab, Bitmap and Grayscale images using Photoshop EPS file format.

Try choosing ASCII or ASCII85 if you experience printing problems or network issues with images saved in Photoshop EPS format.

Select the Include Vector Data checkbox to include vector data such as shapes or type present in the image.

Creating a New File

When you need a fresh, completely blank canvas to work on, you can create a new file.

1 To create a new file, choose File>New. Enter a name for the new document (or leave this as Untitled and do a Save As later).

2 Specify Width and Height settings, or choose dimensions from the Preset menu. If you have copied pixels to the clipboard, the Preset menu is automatically set to Clipboard and the Width and Height entry boxes automatically reflect the dimensions of the elements on the clipboard.

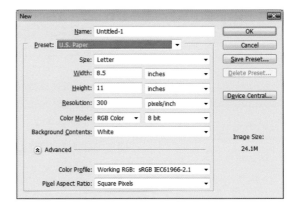

Square Pixels
D1/DV NTSC (0.9)
D4/D16 Standard (0.95)
D1/DV PAL (1.07)
D1/DV NTSC Widescreen (1.2)
HDV 1080/DVCPRO HD 720 (1.33)
D1/DV PAL Widescreen (1.42)
D4/D16 Anamorphic (1.9)
Anamorphic 2:1 (2)
DVCPRO HD 1080 (1.5)

3 Enter a resolution and choose a color mode. You can also specify whether you want to create a file with 1-, 8-, 16- or 32-bits per channel.

4 Select one of the Background Contents options to specify the canvas background you want to begin with, then OK the dialog box.

5 To change the color of the canvas after you click OK in the New dialog box, select a foreground color (see Chapter 4, "Image and Color Basics"). Next, choose Edit>Fill. Choose Foreground Color from the Use pop-up. Make sure Opacity is set to 100% and Mode is Normal. Click OK.

Photomerge

The Photomerge command automates the process of combining two or more images into a panoramic image. The Photomerge command arranges source images based on the overlapping content of each image as well as blending the images to prevent obvious seams where lighting and exposure may vary.

1 Open the images you want to use for the photomerge composition. Choose File>Automate>Photomerge.

2 In the Photomerge dialog box click the Add Open Files button to import the images you want to merge. For best results, leave the Blend Images Together checkbox selected to allow Photoshop to color match images and produce a seamless blend along image borders.

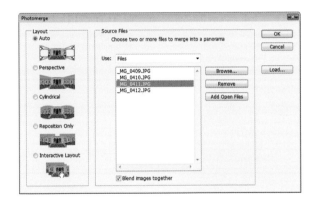

Hot tip

Select the Interactive Layout option if you want to manually align images yourself. If Photoshop is unable to produce a result using any of the other Layout methods the Interactive Layout option opens automatically.

3 Select a Layout Option. Auto typically produces good results. It analyses the images and decides automatically whether Perspective or Cylindrical methods achieve the best result. Select Reposition Only to allow Photoshop to match and align source images, but not transform any image detail.

4 When you click OK Photoshop arranges each source image on a separate layer in a new image window, using layer masks to blend images where they overlap.

Zoomify

An exported Zoomify™ image provides fast download times across the web for high resolution images. It achieves this by dividing the image into a series of tiles which download to provide a seamless end result in the browser. Viewers can zoom and pan to see high quality image detail over the web.

Hot tip

Set up a folder on your hard disk where you want to save the files created by the Zoomify function before you export the image using the Zoomify command.

1 To export an image using Zoomify, choose File> Export>Zoomify.

2 Use the Template pop-up menu to choose a viewer template which sets the background color and navigation controls.

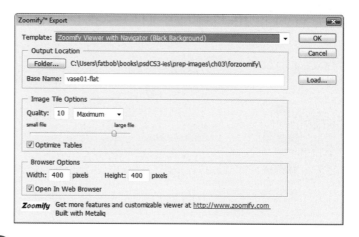

3 Change the Base name if required and specify the location where you want to save the necessary files.

4 Use Image Tile Options to specify the degree of compression and quality for the image tiles.

Don't forget

In order for the zoomify image to preview correctly in a browser, copy all files (the HTML file together with all other files, which are placed in a separate folder) generated by the Zoomify function to your website:

vase01-flat_img   vase01-flat

5 For Browser options specify the width and height of the base image as you want it to appear in the browser. Leave the Open in Browser checkbox selected to preview the results in your default browser. Click OK.

4 Image and Color Basics

This chapter covers a range of basic tasks, such as cropping an image and making it larger or smaller, or changing the resolution to suit your final output needs, that you need to undertake on many of the images on which you work.

Defining colors is another essential aspect of using Photoshop.

Rotating an Image

You can quickly rotate an image if you have scanned it at the wrong orientation, or, for example, if you have imported an image in landscape orientation from a digital camera.

1 To rotate an image in set increments, use Image>Rotate Canvas. Choose one of the preset increments. CW stands for clockwise, CCW for counter-clockwise. In the example above, you would choose 90 degrees clockwise to rotate the image upright.

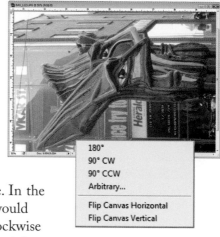

Sometimes you need to adjust an image a few degrees to make up for a poor original photograph or slightly misaligned scan:

2 To rotate in precise amounts, choose Image>Rotate Canvas>Arbitrary. Enter a value for the angle. Choose the clockwise (CW) or counter-clockwise (CCW) radio button, then OK the dialog box.

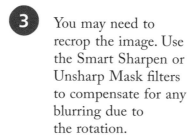

3 You may need to recrop the image. Use the Smart Sharpen or Unsharp Mask filters to compensate for any blurring due to the rotation.

Resizing without Resampling

When you resize an image without resampling, you make the image larger or smaller without changing the total number of pixels in the image. The overall dimensions of the image change, the file size remains the same, but the resolution of the image goes up if you make the image smaller, down if you make the image larger.

Beware

When you make the image smaller without resampling, the pixels get smaller. Effectively, you are increasing the resolution of the image. When you make an image bigger without resampling, the pixels get larger and this can lead to jagged, blocky results. Effectively, you are reducing the resolution of the image.

1 To decrease the size of your image without resampling, choose Image>Image Size. Make sure that Resample Image is deselected. Enter a lower value in the Width or Height entry boxes, or enter a higher resolution. The other measurements update automatically. The file size of the image remains the same – no pixels were added. The resolution has increased – the same number of pixels are packed into a smaller area.

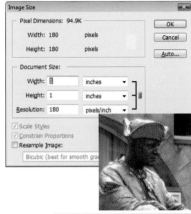

2 To increase the size of your image without resampling, enter a higher value in the Width or Height entry box, or enter a lower resolution. The file size of the image remains the same, but the resolution has decreased.

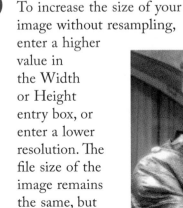

Smaller without resampling

Original

Larger without resampling

Resampling Up

Resampling up involves interpolation. Interpolation is used when Photoshop has to add information – new pixels – that didn't previously exist in an image. Choose an interpolation option from the pop-up in the Image Size dialog box. Bicubic gives best results, but takes longest. Nearest Neighbor is quickest, but least accurate. Bilinear gives a medium quality result. Bicubic Smoother is based on Bicubic, it is intended for enlarging images and can produce smoother results. Bicubic Sharper is useful for reducing the size of images, when preparing them for the Web.

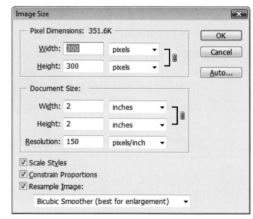

Nearest Neighbor (preserve hard edges)
Bilinear
Bicubic (best for smooth gradients)
Bicubic Smoother (best for enlargement)
Bicubic Sharper (best for reduction)

When you resample up, new pixels are added to the image, so the file size increases. Resampling takes place when you increase the resolution setting, or the width/height settings with the Resample Image option selected. This example starts with a 2in by 2in image at 150 ppi.

1 Choose Image>Image Size. To keep the overall dimensions of the image, but increase the resolution, make sure that Resample Image is selected. Select Constrain Proportions so that the image's original proportions are maintained. Enter a higher value in the Resolution box.

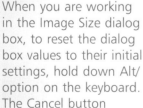
2 The file size and total number of pixels increase, but the Width and Height settings remain the same.

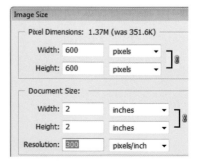

...cont'd

You now have an image which is the same overall size, but which has more pixels in the same area, and therefore its resolution is increased:

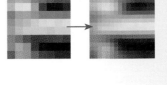

Beware

When you resample an image, blurring may occur due to the process of interpolation. You can use the Smart Sharpen or Unsharp Mask filters to partially compensate for this. (See pages 185–187.)

3 To make the overall dimensions of the image bigger, but to keep the same resolution, again make sure that Resample Image is selected. Select Constrain Proportions to keep width and height proportional. Enter a higher value in either the Width or Height entry boxes. (The other entry box updates automatically if you select Constrain Proportions.)

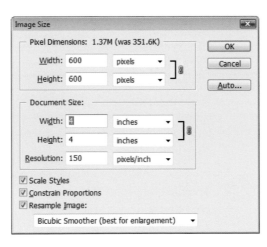

4 The overall dimensions of the image have now increased. The file size and total number of pixels have also increased, but the resolution remains the same.

Sampling Down

Hot tip

Choose View>Print Size to get a representation on screen of the physical size of the image when printed.

You sometimes need to resample down to maintain an optimal balance between the resolution needed for acceptable final output and file size considerations. There is little point in working with an image at too high a resolution if some of the image information is redundant at final output.

Resampling down means discarding pixels. The result is a smaller file size. Resampling down occurs when you decrease the resolution setting, or the width/height settings with the Resample Image option selected.

These examples start with a 2in by 2in image at 300 ppi.

1 Choose Image> Image Size. To keep the overall dimensions of the image, but decrease the resolution, make sure that Resample Image is selected. Leave Constrain Proportions selected, so that the image's original proportions are maintained. Reduce the value in the Resolution box.

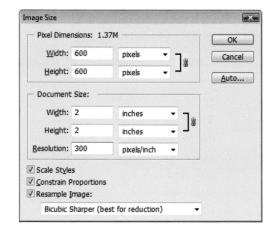

2 The file size goes down and the total number of pixels decreases, whilst the Width and Height settings remain the same.

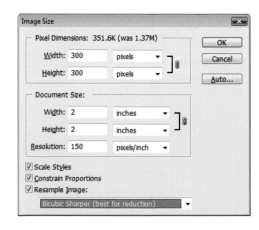

...cont'd

You now have an image which is the same overall size, but with fewer pixels in the same area, and therefore its resolution is lower:

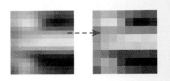

3 To reduce the overall dimensions of the image, but keep the image at the same resolution, make sure that Resample Image is selected. (Select Constrain Proportions to keep the width and height proportional.) Enter a lower value in either the Width or Height entry box. (The other entry box updates automatically if you select Constrain Proportions.)

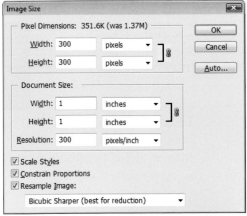

4 The overall dimensions of the image have now decreased. The file size and the total number of pixels have also decreased, but the resolution remains the same.

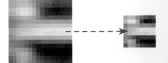

Cropping an Image

Use the Crop tool to crop unwanted areas of an image and reduce the file size.

Hot tip

With a crop marquee active, use the Shield Cropped Area option in the Options bar to hide/show the crop shading overlay. You can also change the color and/or opacity of the crop shading:

1 Select the Crop tool. Position your cursor on the image, then click and drag to define the crop area. Don't worry if you don't get the crop exactly right first time. The area of the image outside the crop dims to indicate the parts of the image to be discarded.

Hot tip

Hold down Shift, then click and drag on a corner handle to resize the crop marquee in proportion.

2 To reposition the crop marquee, place your cursor inside the marquee, then click and drag. To resize the crop marquee, place your cursor on one of the 8 handles around the marquee (the cursor changes to a bi-directional arrow), then click and drag. To rotate the marquee, position your cursor just outside the marquee (the cursor changes shape to indicate rotation), then click and drag in a circular direction.

Hot tip

The Crop tool snaps to the edge of the image. To prevent the snap effect, hold down Ctrl/Command+Shift as you resize the crop marquee.

3 When you are satisfied with the position and size of the crop marquee, click the Commit button in the Options bar, or press Return/Enter to crop the image. Alternatively, you can double-click inside the crop marquee. The areas outside the marquee are discarded. Click the Cancel button, or press the Esc key if you want to remove the crop marquee without cropping.

58

Adding a Border

Borders are useful when you need additional space around the edges of your image.

1 Choose Image>Canvas Size. Use the measurement pop-up menus to choose a unit of measurement. Enter increased values for the Width and/or Height fields.

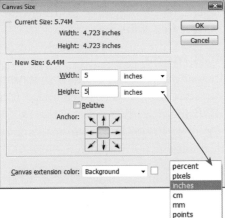

Hot tip

Select the Relative checkbox, then enter a positive or negative number to specify the amount you want to either add to or subtract from the canvas size.

2 To specify where the border is added relative to the image, click one of the placement squares. This sets the relative position of the image and the border. The highlight square represents the position of the image, the other squares the position of the border.

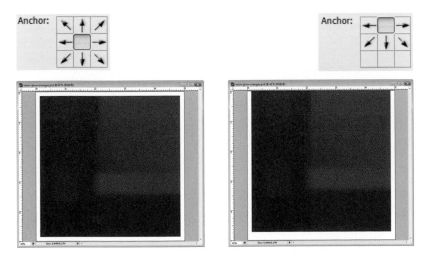

3 Choose a color from the Canvas extension color pop-up menu to specify the color of the border. OK the dialog to add the border. This increases the file size as the command adds pixels to the image.

Image Modes

Image modes are fundamental to working in Photoshop. When you open an image the mode is indicated in the title bar of the image window. There are eight different modes in Photoshop. Use modes as appropriate to your working requirements. Then, depending on output or printing requirements, if necessary, convert to a different mode.

RGB mode

Images are typically scanned or captured in RGB mode. When you start work with a color image it is usually best to work in RGB mode, as this is faster than CMYK mode and allows you to use all of Photoshop's commands and features, providing greatest flexibility.

The disadvantage of working in RGB mode, if your image will be printed commercially, is that RGB allows a greater gamut of colors than you can print. At some stage, some of the brightest, most vibrant colors may lose their brilliance when the image is brought within the CMYK gamut.

CMYK mode

Convert to CMYK when the image is to be printed commercially and you have finished making changes.

To place a color image in a page layout application from where it will be color separated, you need to convert from RGB to CMYK. When you convert from RGB to CMYK, Photoshop adjusts any colors in the RGB image that fall outside the CMYK gamut to their nearest printable color. (See Page 65, for details on gamut warnings.)

You can also select View>Gamut Warning (Ctrl/Command+ Shift+Y), to highlight (in gray) areas of the image that are out of gamut.

Indexed Color mode

This mode reduces your image to 256 colors or less and is frequently used for multimedia and Web images.

Duotone

For details on using Duotone mode see page 62.

Hot tip

To retain the flexibility of working in RGB mode, but see an on-screen CMYK preview of your image, first make sure that View>Proof Setup is set to Working CMYK, then choose View>Proof Colors. (You may have to wait a few seconds when you choose this option as Photoshop builds its color conversion tables.) The title bar of the image changes to indicate that you are working with an RGB image, but previewing in CMYK:

goldman3x3.psd @ 100% (RGB/8/CMYK)

Don't forget

You must first convert to Grayscale mode before you can convert to Bitmap or Duotone mode.

Grayscale mode

When you are not printing an image in color you can convert to Grayscale mode to make working faster and file size smaller.

Lab mode

This mode uses the CIE Lab model which has one channel for luminosity, an "a" channel representing colors blue to yellow and a "b" channel for magenta to green. A significant advantage to this mode is that its gamut encompasses that of both CMYK and RGB modes.

Bitmap mode

This mode reduces everything to black or white pixels. The image becomes a 1-bit image.

Multichannel mode

Multichannel mode uses 256 levels of gray in each channel. When you convert RGB or CMYK images to multichannel mode, the original channels in the image are converted to spot color channels. Multichannel mode is an advanced option – only use it if you have a detailed understanding of the printing process.

1 To convert from one mode to another, choose Image>Mode and choose the mode you want from the sub-menu. Depending on which mode you are converting from and to, you may get a message box warning you of any consequences of converting to the new mode and asking you to confirm your request.

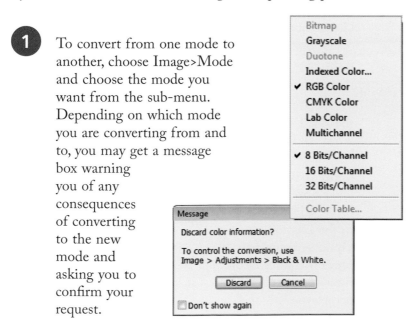

To achieve greater creative flexibility when converting an image to grayscale, choose Image>Adjustments> Black & White. (See page 181 for further information.)

Duotone Mode

Duotone is a very popular effect used to give added tonal depth to a grayscale image by printing with black and another color.

1 To create a duotone, choose Image> Mode>Duotone. Choose from the Type pop-up whether you want to create a duotone (two inks), a tritone (three inks) or a quadtone (four inks).

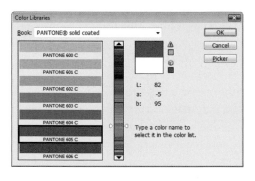

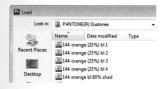

2 To choose a second color for the duotone, click the "Ink 2" color box (below the black ink box). This opens the Color Libraries dialog box. Choose a color. Click the Picker button if you want to use the Color Picker. OK the dialog box.

3 To specify the ink coverage for both colors, click first on the Ink 1 Curve box, then the Ink 2 box. In the Duotone Curve dialog box, drag the curve to the desired position, or enter values in the % entry boxes to adjust the ink coverage curve. Click Preview in the Duotone Options dialog to preview the result in the image window before you OK the dialog boxes.

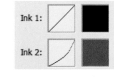

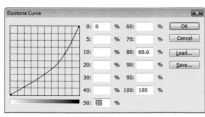

Foreground & Background Colors

The foreground color is applied when you first create type, and when you use the Paint Bucket, Line, Pencil, and Brush tools.

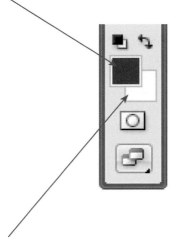

Press X on the keyboard to switch background and foreground colors. Press D on the keyboard to revert to the default foreground and background colors.

The background color is the color you erase to when you use the Eraser tool, or when you delete or move a selection on the Background layer.

When you are working with foreground and background controls you can also switch colors, and you can quickly change back to the default colors, black and white.

You can change the background and foreground colors using the Eyedropper tool, the Color Picker dialog box, the Color palette and the Swatches palette.

1 To switch background to foreground and vice versa, click once on the Switch Colors arrow.

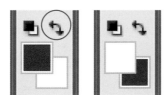

2 To revert to black and white as the default background and foreground colors, click the Default Colors icon.

Eyedropper and Color Sampler

The Eyedropper tool

The Eyedropper tool provides a quick and convenient way to pick up foreground and background color from an area of the image you are working on, or from another inactive Photoshop image window.

1. To set the foreground color, click on the Eyedropper tool. Position your cursor, then click once on the image. The Set foreground color box in the Toolbox now represents the color where you clicked.

2. To set the background color, hold down Alt/option then click on the image. The Set background color box in the Toolbox now indicates the color on which you clicked.

3. To set the Sample Size, use the Sample Size pop-up menu in the Options bar to choose a value. Point Sample reads the precise value of the pixel on which you click. 3 by 3 Average etc. take average values of the pixels where you click.

The Color Sampler tool

Use the Color Sampler tool (with the Info palette) to set up to four sample points which you can refer to as you make adjustments to color values. Each time you click in the image window with the Color Sampler tool, you set a sample point. Each point creates an extra pane in the Info palette. To delete a sample point, drag it out of the image window with the Color Sampler tool.

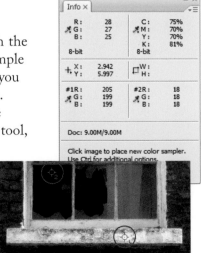

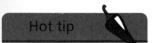

Hot tip

To hide/show the sample points, choose Hide/Show Color Samplers from the Info palette menu.

The Color Picker

Using the Color Picker is a powerful and flexible way of choosing foreground and background colors. You can use a number of different color models to create color.

1 To create a Process color using the Color Picker, click once on either the Set foreground or Set background color box. Enter values in the CMYK

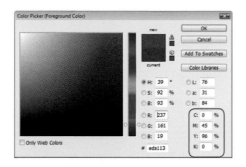

entry boxes. A preview of the color appears in the new color swatch, above the current color swatch.

2 OK the dialog box. The color you defined now becomes the foreground or background color, depending on which box you clicked in Step 1.

You can also create colors using the Color Slider and the Color Field. The next example uses Hue, Saturation and Brightness values. Use the same techniques for RGB and Lab color models.

1 To create a color using Hue, Saturation and Brightness (HSB) values, first click the Hue (H) radio button.

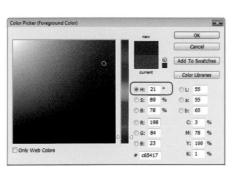

2 Click on the Color Slider bar, or drag the slider triangles on either side of the bar, to choose a hue or color. This sets one of the three HSB values. The number in the Hue entry box represents the hue you have chosen.

Hot tip

Press the Tab key to move the highlight through the entry boxes in the dialog box.

Beware

A warning triangle – the Gamut alarm – appears next to the new/current color boxes if you create a color that cannot be printed using CMYK inks. Click the warning triangle to choose the nearest printable color:

The small box below the warning triangle indicates the nearest printable color.

...cont'd

3 Next, click in the Color Field to set the other two variables – Saturation and Brightness. Clicking to the left of the field reduces the saturation, clicking to the right increases the saturation of the selected hue. Clicking near the bottom decreases brightness, clicking near the top increases brightness for the selected hue.

4 If you click on the Saturation button, the Color Slider now represents saturation (from 0–100) and the Color Field allows you to choose Hue and Brightness values. When you click the Brightness radio button, the slider represents Brightness and the Color Field represents Hue and Saturation.

Choosing Custom Colors

You can access a range of color-matching systems such as PANTONE, Toyo Color Finder and Focoltone Color System using the Color Libraries dialog box.

1 In the Color Picker dialog box, click the Color Libraries button. Use the Book pop-up menu to select a color matching system.

2 If you know the ink number of the color you want, you can enter the number on the keyboard. Alternatively, click in the color slider bar to the right of the ink color boxes. This moves you to a general range of colors. Use the scroll bars at the top and bottom of the sliders to find the specific color you want. Click on the color you want to select, then click OK.

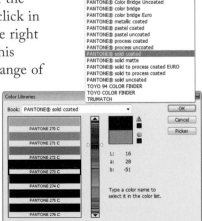

The Color Palette

You can also use the Color palette (Window>Colors) to mix new colors.

1 First identify which color selection box is "active". There are two boxes, Set foreground color and Set background color. The active box is outlined in black.

2 Continue with step 3 if the correct box is active, or click the inactive box to make it the active box if necessary.

3 Drag the Color slider triangles below the Color slider bars, or enter values in the entry boxes to the right of the palette. You can also click on a color in the Color Ramp running along the bottom of the Color palette. The Color Ramp contains every color in the CMYK spectrum as a default setting.

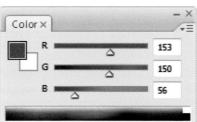

Grayscale Slider
✓ RGB Sliders
HSB Sliders
CMYK Sliders
Lab Sliders
Web Color Sliders

Copy Color as HTML

RGB Spectrum
✓ CMYK Spectrum
Grayscale Ramp
Current Colors

Make Ramp Web Safe

4 Use the palette menu button (⚏) in the top right of the palette to change the color model for the sliders.

5 Choose an option from the bottom half of the palette menu to specify the color model for the colors in the Color Ramp at the bottom of the palette.

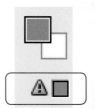
67

The Swatches Palette

You can use the Swatches palette (Window>Swatches) to set foreground and background colors, and you can also use it to create custom palettes which you can save and then reload into a different image.

1 To select a foreground color from the Swatches palette, click on a color swatch. To select a background color, hold down Ctrl/Command and then click on a color swatch.

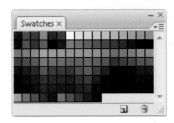

You can customize the Swatches palette by adding and deleting colors in the palette.

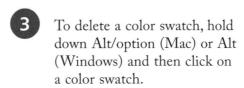

2 To add color to the swatches, select a foreground color. Position your cursor in an empty area of the Swatches palette. (The cursor changes to a paint bucket.) Then click. Enter a name for the new swatch, then click OK to add the current foreground color to the Swatches palette.

3 To delete a color swatch, hold down Alt/option (Mac) or Alt (Windows) and then click on a color swatch.

4 Use the Swatches palette menu ( ) to reset the Swatches palette to its default settings, or to choose a different color palette from the list.

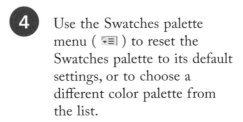

5 The Painting Tools

The painting tools apply color to pixels in an image, and can also be used for editing masks.

The Brush Preset Picker, the Brushes palette and controls available in the Options bar allow you to control all aspects of painting.

The Brush Preset Picker

The Brush Preset Picker allows quick, convenient access to a range of standard, preset brushes.

Rest your cursor on the brush thumbnail in the brush presets scroll box to see a descriptive help label for the tool:

1 To select a brush, click on the Brush tool to select it, then click the Brush pop-up triangle icon in the Options bar.

2 Click on a brush you want to use in the scroll box. A thumbnail icon represents the shape of the brush. The number beneath the brush icon indicates the diameter of the brush in pixels.

For circular shape brushes, use the Hardness slider to increase/decrease the hardness setting for the edge of the brush. (See page 76 for further information on setting Hardness).

3 To change the size of the brush, drag the Master Diameter slider to increase/decrease the size of the brush, or enter a value in pixels in the diameter entry box. Click the Use Sample Size button to return to the original size of the brush if you have made changes to the Master Diameter. (This option is only available for brush tip shapes created originally from a sample of pixels).

4 Create settings for Mode, Opacity and Flow in the Options bar and choose the Airbrush option if required.

To constrain your painting strokes to straight lines, click with the Painting tool to position the start of the stroke, move your cursor (do not click and drag) then hold down Shift and click to end the stroke.

5 Position your cursor in the image window, then click and drag to apply the foreground color using the current brush characteristics and the brush settings in the Options bar.

Opacity

Opacity (Brush, Pencil, History Brush, Art History Brush, Gradient, Paint Bucket, Clone Stamp and Pattern Stamp tools) controls how completely pixels are covered with the foreground color when you drag across them.

Make sure the Opacity slider is at 100% if you want to completely cover the pixels you drag across. (Soft-edged brushes only partially cover pixels around the edge of the painting stroke to create the soft edge effect.) Reducing the Opacity setting gives less complete results in the area you drag across, creating a semi-transparent, partially-covered effect.

Hot tip

Remember to choose the foreground color you want to paint with before you start to use a painting tool.

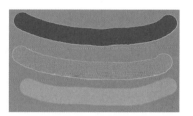

100%

60%

20%

Flow

Flow controls how quickly paint is applied when you drag the brush across the image.

Hot tip

For a description of blending modes, see pages 81–83.

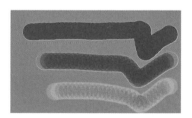

100%

60%

20%

Airbrush

Select the Airbrush option to imitate the effect of spraying paint with an airbrush. The Airbrush option works best with soft-edged brushes and reduced Opacity and Flow settings.

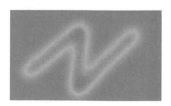

Brush: 90px Soft Edge
Opacity: 80%
Flow: 40%

Don't forget

The Airbrush option is selected when the icon in the Options bar has a border around it:

71

The Brushes Palette

The Brushes palette provides access to a wide variety of options for controlling the appearance and characteristics of your brush strokes. You can use preset brushes, or you can create your own custom brushes using a variety of interchangeable settings.

1 To create custom brush characteristics, select a painting tool. By default, the Brushes palette is located in the Palette dock (on the right-hand side of the Photoshop window). Click on the Brushes icon to display the Brushes palette.

2 Make sure the Brush Presets option is selected. Click on a preset brush in the scroll list. You can rest your cursor on a preset brush in the scroll list to show a help label which indicates the settings currently applied to the 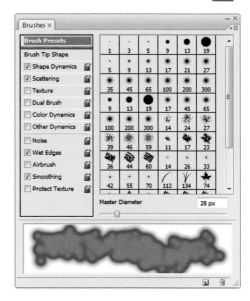 brush. Depending on the brush preset you click on, the various customized settings already applied to the brush, visible in the left hand column, change accordingly.

3 To customize the preset brush by adding your own brush settings, click the checkboxes to the left of the brush characteristic labels. The preview pane at the bottom of the palette updates to indicate the effect on the brush. (In this example the 13-pixel, soft-edged brush is selected, with Scattering, Shape Dynamics, Smoothing, Wet Edges and Master Diameter also applied.)

4 Drag the Diameter slider to change the size of the brush, or enter a value in pixels in the entry box.

5 Click on the
Brush Tip
Shape button
to change
shape settings
such as Angle,
Roundness,
Hardness
and Spacing
if required.
(See page 76
for further
information.)

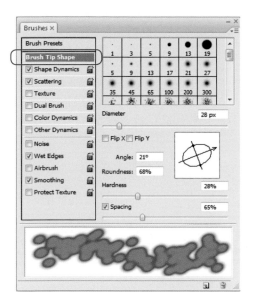

Beware

Selecting the Airbrush
option in the Options
palette is the equivalent
of selecting Airbrush
from the effects list in
the Brushes palette.

6 Click the brush
characteristic
label (to the
right of the check box) to access a range of controls for
the option. (See page 74 for information on creating
custom brush characteristic settings.)

7 Create settings for Mode, Opacity and Flow in the
Options bar.

8 If you click on a different brush
in the scroll list, any custom
settings for the previously
selected brush are lost. Create
a tool preset if you want to
save the settings on a more
permanent basis. (See page 78 for
further information.)

Don't forget

Use the Brush Presets
Picker palette when you
want to quickly select a
brush from the existing
set of brushes. Use the
Brushes palette to select
a preset brush and also
to create and design your
own custom brushes.

9 Position your cursor in the image
window, then click and drag to
create the required paint stroke.

Custom Brush Settings

To understand what Photoshop refers to as paint marks, select a simple preset brush, click the Brush Tip Shape button, then drag the spacing slider to the right. This indicates visually how the individual paint marks form a paint stroke when you drag the Brush tool in the image window.

Preset brushes can be customized using the style options on the left side of the Brushes palette together with the settings which control the Brush Tip Shape. Effects above the gray divider bar have controls that allow you to customize each effect. Style options below the gray divider bar cannot be edited.

1 To create custom settings for a brush effect such as Shape Dynamics, click the effect label (the words Shape Dynamics) – not the checkbox. The controls available for each brush effect appear on the right of the dialog box.

2 Experiment with the settings available. The preview box at the bottom of the palette updates to reflect changes you make to the settings.

Shape Dynamics

The Shape Dynamics options control the manner in which brush marks in the painting stroke change as you drag your cursor in the image window.

Scattering

Scattering settings allow you to specify how the position of the paint marks in a stroke is varied and also control the number of paint marks in a stroke.

Texture

Use texture settings on a brush to associate the brush with a pattern to create paint strokes that appear to be painted on a textured canvas.

Dual Brush

Dual Brush uses two tips to create the brush stroke. Set options for the primary tip using options in the Brush Tip Shape area. Set options for the secondary tip in the Dual Brush area.

Color Dynamics

Color Dynamics settings control how the color of the painting stroke changes over the length of the stroke.

Other Dynamics

Other Dynamics control the speed with which paint is applied and the opacity of the paint in the stroke.

Noise

Noise has the most apparent effect around the edges of soft-edged brushes and creates a random scattering of pixels.

Wet Edges

Wet Edges creates a stroke that is darker around the edges and translucent inside the stroke, imitating the uneven build up of paint in a watercolor.

Airbrush

The Airbrush option on a soft-edged brush with a medium to low Opacity setting simulates the effect of spraying paint with an airbrush.

Smoothing

Smoothing helps create smoother curves in brush strokes.

Protect Texture

Select the Protect Texture option to keep texture effects consistent when painting with different textured brush tips. The option applies the same pattern and scale to all preset brushes with a texture.

Brush Tip Shape Settings

The Brush Tip Shape options area of the Brushes palette provides further controls for specifying the appearance of a brush stroke.

 1 To create custom brush tip shape settings for a brush, first select a brush from the Brush Presets list. Then click the Brush Tip Shape button in the Brushes palette. Enter values for Diameter, Hardness, Spacing, Angle and Roundness in the brush tip settings area.

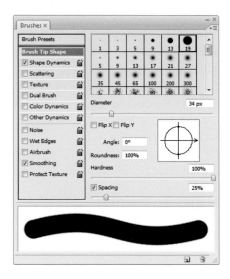

Hot tip

To save custom brush tip settings for future use, see page 78 – "Creating Brush Preset Tools".

Diameter

Enter a value in pixels for the diameter of your brush from 1–2500. Brush sizes too large to be represented at their actual size will display with the diameter indicated as a number.

Hardness

A setting of 100% gives a hard-edged brush. Lower settings produce soft-edged brushes. The lower you take this setting, the more diffuse the resultant stroke when you paint with the brush. Even with settings of 100%, the edge of the brush-stroke is anti-aliased.

Spacing

Spacing is measured as a percentage of brush size. 25% is the default setting for standard brushes. Higher settings begin to create non-continuous strokes.

Angle and Roundness

Use these controls together to create a stroke which thickens and thins like a calligraphic pen. You can enter values in the entry boxes, or drag the arrow indicator to change the angle, and drag the diameter dots to change the diameter.

Hot tip

Select the Flip X or Flip Y checkbox to flip the paint mark across its vertical or horizontal axis to change the direction of the brush effect.

The Pencil Tool

You can use the Pencil tool to draw freeform lines. The lines you draw with the Pencil tool are always hard-edged – in other words, the edges of your lines are not anti-aliased. The Pencil tool paints or draws with the foreground color.

1 To draw a line, first select the Pencil tool. Set a brush size using the Brush Preset Picker. (See page 70.) Or use the Brushes palette to create custom brush settings for the tool. (See page 72.)

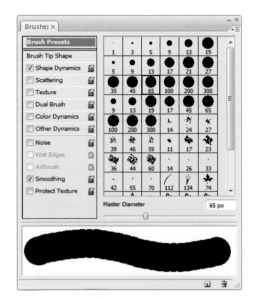

2 Use the Pencil Options bar to specify: Blending Mode, Opacity and Auto Erase options.

3 Click and drag to create a freeform pencil stroke. Hold down Shift, then drag to constrain the pencil stroke vertically or horizontally.

4 To create a straight pencil stroke between two points, click, move the cursor to a new position (do not click and drag), hold down Shift, then click again.

Auto Erase
Select this checkbox to use the Pencil tool to paint out or erase areas of foreground color using the current background color.

Creating Brush Preset Tools

Create a Brush tool preset when you have created custom brush settings that you want to be able to reuse, without having to first recreate the custom settings.

1 To create a Brush tool preset, select the Brush tool, then use the Brushes palette to create custom settings for the brush.

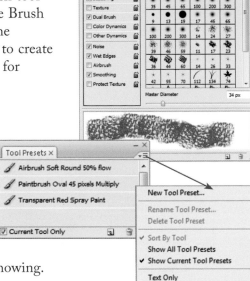

2 Click the Tool Presets icon in the Palette dock, to show the palette if it is not already showing.

3 Choose New Tool Preset from the palette menu (≡). Enter a name for the tool preset in the New Tool Preset dialog box.

4 To access the new tool preset, make sure you have the Brush tool selected, then click the Brush tool presets triangle in the Options bar. Click on the tool preset in the drop-down list.

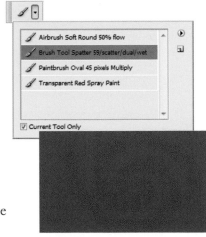

78

The Gradient Tool

You can use the Gradient tool to create transitions from one color to another. You can also create multicolored gradients. There are options for Linear, Radial, Angle, Reflected and Diamond gradients. You can apply a gradient fill to a selection, or to an entire active layer.

1 To create a gradient fill, select the Gradient tool. Choose a gradient type from the Options bar.

2 Select a Blending mode and set Opacity. Use the Gradient pop-up to choose one of the preset gradients.

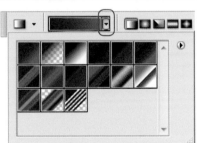

Hot tip

Hold down Shift as you click and drag to constrain a linear gradient to 45° increments.

3 Position your cursor where you want the gradient to start, then click and drag. The angle and distance you drag the cursor defines the angle and distance of a linear gradient, or the radius of a radial gradient. (Click and drag from the center out to create Radial, Angle, Reflected and Diamond gradient fills.)

4 For basic gradient fills you can leave the Transparency and Dither options selected. Choose the Reverse option to reverse the order of the colors in the gradient.

Hot tip

For a linear gradient, the start and end colors fill any part of the selection that you do not drag the cursor across. For radial gradients, the end color fills the remaining area.

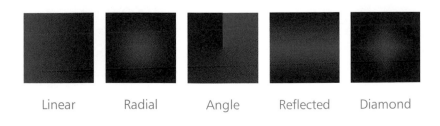

Linear   Radial   Angle   Reflected   Diamond

The Paint Bucket Tool

You can use the Paint Bucket tool to color pixels with the foreground color, based on a tolerance setting. It works in a similar way to the Magic Wand tool, but in this case filling adjoining pixels that fall within the tolerance setting. You can use the Paint Bucket tool within a selection or on the entire image.

Don't forget

The Anti-aliased option creates a slightly soft edge in the areas that the Paint Bucket fills.

Beware

You cannot use the Paint Bucket on images in Bitmap mode.

80

1 To fill an area with the foreground color, select the Paint Bucket tool. Leave the Fill pop-up set to Foreground. Enter a value from 0–255 in the Tolerance box. The higher you set the value, the greater the pixel range the Paint Bucket fills.

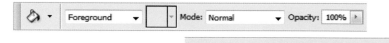

2 Set Opacity, Blending mode, Anti-aliased and All Layers options as required. Position your cursor then click on the image.

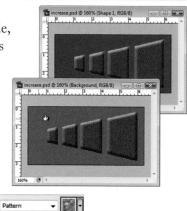

3 You can use the Paint Bucket to fill with a pattern previously saved into the pattern library. Use the Fill pop-up to choose Pattern, then use the Pattern pop-up palette to choose an available pattern.

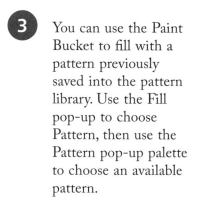

4 Deselect the Contiguous option to allow the Paint Bucket to color pixels anywhere in the image, provided that they fall within the Tolerance setting.

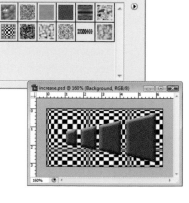

Blending Modes

Choose blending modes from the pop-up menu in the Options bar for each painting tool. The various paint modes in combination with opacity/pressure settings have a selective control on which pixels are affected when you use the painting and editing tools. The result is more of a blending of the paint color and the color of the base pixels than simply one color replacing another.

Dissolve
Produces a grainy, chalk-like effect. Not all pixels are colored as you drag across the image, leaving gaps and holes in the stroke. Reduce the Opacity setting to control the effect.

Clear
Makes pixels transparent. You can only access this mode on a layer with the Lock Transparency option deselected. Available for the Brush, Paint Bucket, Pencil and Line tools.

Behind
Only available when you are working on a layer with a transparent background. Make sure Lock Transparency is deselected for the layer. Use Behind to paint behind the existing pixels on a layer. Paint appears in the transparent areas, but does not affect the existing pixels.

Darken
Applies the paint color to pixels that are lighter than the paint color – doesn't change pixels darker than the paint color.

Multiply
Combines the color you are painting with the color of the pixels you drag across, to produce a color that is darker than the original colors.

Color Burn
Darkens the base color by increasing the contrast in base color pixels, depending on the blend color. More pronounced when paint color is dark. Blending with white has no effect.

Don't forget

The blending modes allow you to make changes to an image using the painting and editing tools in a more selective and subtle way than simply painting with the foreground color. The color you paint with (the blend color) combines with the color of the pixels you drag across (the base color) to produce a different color depending on the blending mode you select.

Hot tip

Refer to the original image below for comparison purposes. This image uses Normal blending mode:

Don't forget

Blending modes are also available in the Layers palette and in the Fill Path, Fill, Stroke and Fade dialog boxes.

Linear Burn

Darkens the base color by decreasing brightness depending on the blend color used. Blending with white has no effect.

Lighten

Replaces pixels darker than the paint color, but does not change pixels lighter than the paint color.

Screen

Produces the opposite effect to Multiply. It multiplies the opposite of the original color by the painting color and has the effect of lightening the pixels.

Color Dodge

Brightens the base color by decreasing contrast. More pronounced when the paint color is light. Blending with black has no effect.

Linear Dodge

Brightens the base color by increasing the brightness depending on the blend color. Blending with black has no effect.

Overlay

This increases the contrast and saturation, combining the foreground color with the pixels you drag across. Highlights and shadows in the base color are preserved.

Soft Light

Creates a soft lighting effect. Lightens colors if the painting color is lighter than 50% gray, darkens colors if the painting color is darker than 50% gray.

Hard Light

Multiplies (darkens) or screens (lightens) pixels, depending on the paint color, and tends to increase contrast.

...cont'd

Vivid Light
Burns or Dodges base pixel colors by increasing or decreasing contrast depending on the blend color.

Linear Light
Burns or Dodges base pixel colors by increasing or decreasing brightness depending on the blend color.

Pin Light
Replaces base color pixels depending on whether the blend color is lighter or darker than 50% gray.

Difference
Examines the brightness of pixels and the paint color, then subtracts paint brightness from pixel brightness. Depending on the result, it inverts the pixels.

Exclusion
The result is similar to Difference, but with lower contrast.

Hue
In color images, applies the hue (color) of the paint, without affecting the saturation or luminosity of the base pixels.

Saturation
Changes the saturation of pixels based on the saturation of the blend color, but does not affect hue or luminosity.

Luminosity
Changes the relative lightness/darkness of the pixels without affecting their hue or saturation.

Color
Applies the hue and saturation of the blend color; does not affect base pixel luminosity.

Hot tip

To constrain your painting strokes to straight lines, click with the Painting tool to position the start of the stroke, move your cursor (do not click and drag) then hold down Shift and click to end the stroke.

Creating Rasterized Shapes

A rasterized shape is a shape comprised of pixels. It is not based on a vector path and cannot be edited in the same way as a shape layer.

1 To create a rasterized shape, select a layer, or create a new layer. Select a foreground color for the shape.

	Rectangle Tool	U
Rounded Rectangle Tool	U
Ellipse Tool	U
Polygon Tool	U
Line Tool	U
Custom Shape Tool	U

2 Select either the Rectangle, Rounded Rectangle, Ellipse, Line, Polygon or Custom Shape tool.

3 Select the Fill Pixels button in the Options bar.

4 Position your cursor in the image window. Drag diagonally to define the size of the shape. The shape appears in the window. It does not automatically create a new layer. A rasterized shape is the equivalent of creating a selection, then filling it with a color.

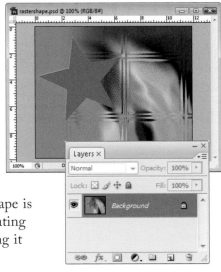

5 For each of the Shape tools you can create custom settings. Click the Geometry Options pop-up triangle to the right of the Custom Shape tool. Each tool has its own specific set of controls.

Polygon Options
Radius:
☐ Smooth Corners
☑ Star
Indent Sides By: 50%
☐ Smooth Indents

6 The Editing Tools

The editing tools covered in this chapter let you edit or change pixels in a variety of ways. The tools can be used within a selection or anywhere on an image. Many of the techniques and keyboard shortcuts covered for the painting tools apply to the editing tools as well.

Blur, Sharpen and Smudge

The Blur and Sharpen Tools

The Blur and Sharpen tools are the two "focus" tools. The Blur tool works by reducing contrast between pixels and can be useful for disguising unwanted, jagged edges and softening edges between shapes. The Sharpen tool works by increasing the contrast between pixels.

1 To blur or sharpen areas of your image, select the appropriate tool. In the Options bar, set the Blend mode, Strength and Use All Layers options, position your cursor on the image, then click and drag to blur or sharpen the pixels. Release the mouse then drag across the pixels again to intensify the effect. You may produce a coarse, grainy effect if you overuse the Sharpen tool. Use a low Strength setting and build up the effect gradually.

The Smudge Tool

Use the Smudge tool to create an effect similar to dragging your finger through wet paint. The Smudge tool picks up color from where you start to drag and smears it into adjacent colors.

1 Select the Smudge tool. Set the Strength, position your cursor on the image, then start to drag to smudge the colors. The higher the Strength setting, the more pronounced the effect.

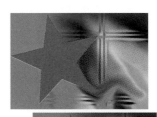

2 Select the Finger Painting option to begin the smudge with the current foreground color. Select the Use All Layers option to smudge colors from other layers in the image onto the layer you are working on. Leave this option deselected if you want the smudge to pick up color from pixels on the active layer only.

The Clone Stamp Tool

You can use the Clone Stamp tool to retouch an image by cloning or duplicating areas of pixels. This is very useful when you want to remove blemishes and scratches.

1 To clone an area of an image, select the Clone Stamp tool. Set an appropriate brush size using the Brush Preset Picker in the Options bar. Make sure Aligned is selected.

2 Hold down Alt/option and click on the part of the image you want to clone.

3 Release Alt/option. Move the cursor to a different image part then click and drag. The pixels in the image where you drag are replaced by pixels cloned from the spot where you first clicked. A crosshair at the point where you first clicked indicates the pixels that are being cloned – the source point.

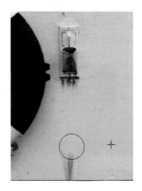

Clone – Aligned
With Aligned selected, the distance from the source point (shown by the crosshair) to the Clone Stamp cursor remains fixed. When you release the mouse, move the cursor, then continue to use the Clone Stamp tool, the relative position of the source point and the Clone Stamp cursor remains constant, but you will now clone pixels from a different part of the image.

Clone – Non-aligned
With the Aligned option off, the source point – where you first click – remains the same. If you stop dragging with the Clone Stamp cursor, move to a different part of the image, then start dragging again, the pixels you clone continue to come from the original source point.

Hot tip

Use the "[" or "]" keys on the keyboard to decrease/increase the size of editing tool brushes as you work.

Hot tip

Select which layers you want to include in the clone sample from the Sample pop-up menu. Click the Ignore Adjustment Layers button to exclude Adjustment layers from the sample:

Dodge, Burn and Sponge

Don't forget

You cannot use the Dodge, Burn or Saturate/Desaturate tools on an image in Bitmap or Indexed Color mode.

The Dodge, Burn, Saturate/Desaturate group of tools are sometimes referred to as the "toning" tools. The Dodge and Burn tools are based on the traditional photographic technique of decreasing the amount of exposure given to a specific area on a print to lighten it (dodging), or increasing the exposure to darken areas (burning-in).

The Dodge and Burn Tools

Use the Dodge tool to lighten pixels in your image; the Burn tool to darken pixels in your image.

1 To lighten or darken areas of an image, select the appropriate tool. Remember to choose a suitable brush size. A soft-edged brush usually creates the smoothest result.

Hot tip

It's a good idea to use a low exposure setting when you lighten areas of an image so that you build up the effect gradually.

2 In the Options bar, set the Range pop-up menu to Midtones, Shadows or Highlights to limit changes to the middle range of grays, the dark or light areas of the image respectively, and also set Exposure to control the intensity of the tool.

3 Position your cursor on the image, then click and drag to lighten/darken the pixels. Release the mouse then drag across the pixels again to intensify the effect.

The Sponge Tool

You can use the Sponge tool when you want to subtly increase or decrease color saturation in areas of your image.

Don't forget

Each Toning tool retains its own settings when you switch to another tool in the same group.

1 To saturate/desaturate areas of an image, select the Sponge tool. Remember to select an appropriate brush size. Set the Mode pop-up to Saturate or Desaturate. Position your cursor on the image, then click and drag to alter the saturation.

The Eraser Tool

Use the Eraser tool to erase portions of your image. The Eraser rubs out to the background color when you are working on the Background layer. It erases to transparency when you are working on any other layer, provided that the Transparency Lock option is not selected in the Layers palette.

Don't forget

Use the Master Diameter setting in the Brush Preset Picker palette to specify the Eraser size when using the tool in Brush and Pencil mode.

1 To erase areas of your image, select the Eraser tool to show Eraser options in the Options bar. Use the bar to specify brush size, Mode, Opacity, Flow, Airbrush and Erase to History options.

2 Click and drag on your image to erase to the background color or transparency, depending on the layer on which you are working.

Opacity
Use the Opacity setting to create the effect of partially erasing pixels in the image.

Mode
Use the Mode pop-up to choose an erase mode. The default is Brush. Block is useful when you need to erase along straight edges. The Block eraser is a fixed-size square.

Erase to History
Use the Erase to History option to return pixels to their status at a particular state in the History palette. Click in the History Brush column in the History palette to set the state to which the Erase to History option returns pixels.

Hot tip

Hold down Alt/option with the Eraser tool selected to access the Erase to History option temporarily. Click and drag across modified areas of the image to restore them to the specified state in the History palette.

The Magic Eraser

Use the Magic Eraser tool to erase pixels on a layer to transparency. The Magic Eraser works best when you want to remove the background pixels around a hard-edged object. The Magic Eraser tool erases pixels based on a tolerance level, similar to the way in which the Magic Wand works. (See page 103 for information on the Magic Wand.)

1 To use the Magic Eraser tool, first select the layer on which you want to work. Select the Magic Eraser tool to show the Magic Eraser options in the Options bar. Enter a Tolerance value. Set a low Tolerance value to erase pixels that are very similar in color value to the pixel on which you first click. Set a high Tolerance value to select a wider range of pixels.

2 Set an Opacity value of 100% to erase pixels completely. Set a lower Opacity value to create a partially transparent effect. Select the Anti-aliased option to create a smoother edge when pixels are erased. (See page 99 for further information on anti-aliasing.)

3 Select Contiguous to erase only pixels that fall within the Tolerance value specified, and that are adjacent to each other. This option erases continuous areas of pixels. Deselect Contiguous if you want the Magic Eraser to erase all pixels that fall within the Tolerance value anywhere in the image.

4 Position the cursor, then click to erase pixels that fall within the Tolerance value.

The Background Eraser

Use the Background Eraser tool when you are working on a layer to erase pixels to transparency. You can set tolerance and sampling values to control the level of transparency and the sharpness of its boundary edges.

1 To erase pixels on a layer, select a layer on which you want to work. Select the Background Eraser tool to show its options in the Options bar. Select a brush from the Brush Presets picker.

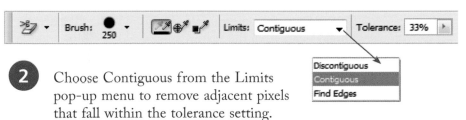

2 Choose Contiguous from the Limits pop-up menu to remove adjacent pixels that fall within the tolerance setting. (Discontiguous erases pixels throughout the image, Find Edges preserves sharp edges along objects).

3 Enter a Tolerance value, or drag the Tolerance slider. Set a low Tolerance value to limit the effect to pixels that are very similar in color value to pixels at the "hotspot". Set a high Tolerance value to erase a broader range of similar colors.

4 Choose a Sampling option. Select Continuous to erase all colors that you drag across. Select Once to erase pixels that are the same color as the pixel on which you first click. This is useful when you want to erase areas of solid color. Select Background Swatch to erase areas containing the current background color.

5 Position your cursor, then click or drag to erase pixels on the layer to transparency, based on the settings you have chosen.

Select the Protect Foreground Color checkbox in the options bar to prevent the tool from erasing pixels that match the current foreground color.

Don't forget

A crosshair at the center of the brush cursor indicates the tool's "hotspot" – the point at which the tool's settings have the greatest effect. The strength of the effect diminishes further away from the hotspot:

The Healing Brush Tool

Use the Healing Brush tools to correct flaws and imperfections in an image. The Healing Brush is similar to the Clone Stamp tool in the way it works, but it also matches the texture, luminosity and shading of the sampled pixels to the pixels in the area you want to "heal", producing a smooth, seamless result.

1 To "heal" an imperfection, select the Healing Brush tool. Use the Brush Preset Picker palette to choose a brush size. Select a blending mode if required. Use Replace mode to preserve the texture, noise and any film grain at the edges of the brush strokes. Leave the Source option set to Sampled to use pixels from within the image.

2 Select Aligned in the Options bar (see page 87 for information on the Aligned option).

3 Position your cursor on an area of the image that you want to sample from in order to repair the imperfection. Hold down Alt/option, then click the mouse button. This sets the sample area of pixels.

Hot tip

See page 96 for information on using the Healing Brush tool in conjunction with the Clone Source palette.

4 Release the Alt/option key. Move your cursor over the area you want to repair. Click, or press and drag to repair the area. When you click or drag the mouse, the (+) indicates the area of the image you are sampling pixels from.

The Spot Healing Brush Tool

Like the Healing Brush tool, the Spot Healing Brush tool removes unwanted detail and repairs imperfections in an image. It typically works best on fairly small areas of detail. The Spot Healing Brush does not require you to set a sample point, it automatically samples pixels in the area of the brush.

1 Select the tool, then select a brush size large enough to cover the blemish.

2 Position your cursor on the blemish, then click once to remove it. If necessary you can click and drag over the blemish. The Spot Healing brush matches the shading, luminosity, texture and transparency of pixels to remove the unwanted detail.

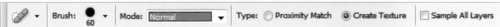

3 For the Spot Healing Brush, the Proximity Match option available in the Options bar samples pixels around the tool cursor in order to adjust texture luminosity, shading and transparency values to remove the blemish. Create Texture analyses pixels in the area of the brush to create a texture that replaces the blemish.

The Patch Tool

The Patch tool allows you to disguise problems and flaws in an image by cloning or copying pixels from another, similar part of the image. The Patch tool attempts to match the texture and shading of the pixels that are copied or sampled to the source pixels – the pixels you are patching over.

1 Select the Patch tool. Select Source in the Options bar. Drag in the image to select the area of pixels you want to patch over.

2 Still working with the Patch tool, position your cursor inside the Patch selection, then drag the selection area onto the area of the image from which you want to copy pixels.

3 Release the mouse button. The original patch selection is repaired with pixels sampled from the area you released on.

4 Alternatively, select Destination in the Options Bar to reverse the way in which the tool works. Use the Patch tool to select the area of pixels you want to use to make the repair. Drag the Patch selection onto the area of pixels you want to repair. Release the mouse to copy the initial selection area over the flaw.

Hot tip

To fix "red eye" caused by camera flash, select the Red Eye tool, position your cursor on the red eye in the image, then click.

In most instances the default settings work well. Adjust Pupil Size and Darken Pupil settings in the Options bar if necessary:

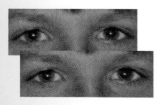

Color Replacement Tool

Use the Color Replacement tool to paint over specific colors in an image.

1 To paint over a color, select the Color Replacement tool. Select a foreground color. Create settings such as Diameter using the Brush Preset picker in the Options bar. Leave Mode set to Color.

2 For Sampling, choose Continuous to sample and replace colors continuously as you drag. Choose Once to replace only the target color you first click on. This makes the tool very specific and typically changes only a limited number of pixels. Choose Background Swatch to limit color changes to pixels that are the same color as the Background color.

3 From the Limits drop down menu choose Contiguous to color pixels immediately adjacent to the pixels you drag across and that fall within the Tolerance setting. Choose Discontiguous to color pixels anywhere within the brush diameter, even if the pixels are not immediately adjacent to the pixels you drag across. Choose Find Edges to help preserve sharpness along edge detail as you replace color.

4 Position your cursor on the pixels you want to change. The Color Replacement tool displays a crosshair at the center of the brush cursor. This indicates the tool's "hotspot" – the point at which the tool's settings have the greatest effect. Click and drag to paint over the pixels.

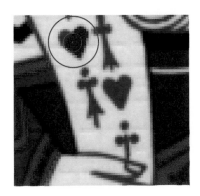

95

Hot tip

Leave the Anti-aliased option selected to achieve a smooth edge to the areas where you replace color:

Hot tip

Enter a Tolerance amount, or drag the Tolerance slider to set a Tolerance value. Set a low value to limit changes to pixels that are very similar in color to the pixels at the center of the brush. Set a high value to color a broader range of pixels:

Clone Source Palette

Use the Clone Source palette to specify and control up to 5 clone sources for use with the Clone Stamp and Healing Brush tools. You can rotate and scale clone sources as well as showing an overlay of the clone source as you edit the image.

1 To set a clone source point that you can return to as you work on an image, select the Clone Stamp tool or the Healing Brush tool. Set an appropriate brush size. (See pages 70–76 for information on working with brushes.)

2 In the Clone Source palette (Window>Clone Source) click the first Clone source button to make it active. Position your cursor over the pixels in the image that you want to use as the source pixels. Hold down the Alt/option key – the cursor changes ( ) – click to set the clone source point. You can repeat this process for the 4 remaining clone source points.

3 Use the W/H entry boxes to scale the source pixels you clone and the rotate ( ) box to change the angle of the pixels you clone.

4 It can sometimes be helpful to see an overlay of the clone source pixels you are sampling as you paint with the Clone Stamp or Healing Brush tool. To do this, select the Show Overlay checkbox and if necessary adjust the Opacity.

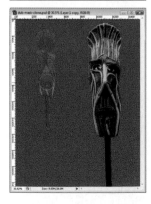

7 Selections

One of the most important techniques when using Photoshop is making selections. When you make a selection, you are selecting an area of the image to which you want to make changes, and isolating the remainder of the image so that it is not affected by changes. A selection is indicated on-screen by a dotted selection marquee.

Marquee Selection Tools

The Marquee selection tools allow you to drag with the mouse to make selections. You can make rectangular or elliptical selections by choosing the appropriate tool.

1 To make a rectangular or oval selection, choose the Rectangular or Elliptical Marquee tool.

2 Position your cursor on the image, then click and drag to define the area you want to select. When you release the cursor you will see a dotted rectangular or oval marquee defining the area of the selection.

3 Hold down Shift, then click and drag with the Rectangular or Elliptical Marquee tool to create a square or circular selection. Hold down Alt/option to create a selection from the center out. Hold down Alt+Shift, to create a square or circular selection from the center out.

4 You can reposition the selection marquee if you need to. Make sure the Marquee tool is still selected, position your cursor inside the selection marquee (the cursor changes shape), then click and drag. You can move selection marquees with any of the Selection tools.

5 With the Marquee tool selected, you can deselect a selection by clicking inside or outside the selection marquee. Alternatively, you can choose Select>Deselect (Ctrl/Command+D).

Marquee Options

You can use the Marquee Options bar to make changes to the way in which the Marquee tools work.

1 Select the Rectangular or Elliptical Marquee tool. Make sure the New Selection button is selected in the Options bar.

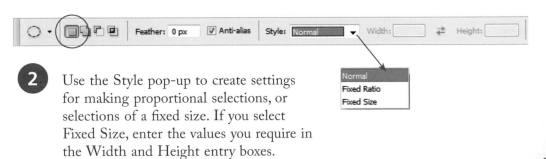

2 Use the Style pop-up to create settings for making proportional selections, or selections of a fixed size. If you select Fixed Size, enter the values you require in the Width and Height entry boxes.

3 The Anti-aliased option is an important control when using bitmap applications such as Photoshop. Select Anti-aliased to create a slightly blurred, soft edge around the selection and the pixels that surround the selection. Using Anti-aliased helps avoid creating unwanted jagged edges.

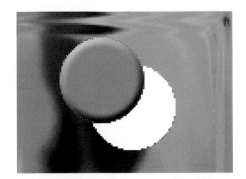

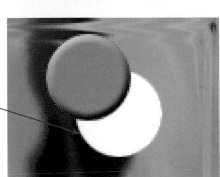

4 Use the Feather or Refine Edge commands to create a soft, feathered edge. (See pages 105–106 in this chapter.)

Don't forget

The Anti-aliased option is also available in the Lasso and Magic Wand Options bars.

Hot tip

Choose Select>Reselect to reselect your most recent selection. You can use the Reselect command even if you have performed operations and commands on the image since you deselected.

Moving Selected Pixels

You can use the Selection tools to reposition a selection border, but you must use the Move tool if you want to move pixels from one location to another.

1 Make a selection. Select the Move tool, then position your cursor inside the Marquee selection border. Click and drag to move the selected pixels.

When you move pixels on the Background layer, the area from which the pixels are moved fills with the current background color. As long as the selection border remains selected, you can continue to move the pixels. Whilst the selection is active, the pixels in the selection "float" above the underlying pixels, without replacing them.

2 To "defloat" the pixels so that they replace the underlying pixels, choose Select>Deselect if you have the Move tool or Magic Wand tool selected. If you used Ctrl/Command with a Marquee or Lasso tool selected, click outside the selection marquee. As soon as you deselect, the pixels on the Background layer that were underneath the floating selection – the underlying pixels – are completely replaced by the pixels in the floating selection.

3 To move a selection and make a copy of it at the same time, hold down Alt/option before you drag with the Move tool. The cursor turns into a double-headed arrow, indicating that you are copying the selection.

4 You can turn a "floating" selection into a layer by choosing Layer>New>Layer Via Cut/Layer Via Copy. (See Chapter 8, "Layers".)

The Lasso Tools

You can use the Lasso tool to make freeform selections by clicking and dragging. It is a useful tool for selecting irregular areas and for quickly adding to or subtracting from selections made with other selection tools, such as the Magic Wand tool.

1 Select the Lasso tool. Set Feather and Anti-aliased options. Position your cursor on the image. The cursor changes to the Lasso cursor. Click and drag around the part of the image you want to select. Make sure your cursor comes back to the start point. If you release before reaching the start point, Photoshop completes the selection with a straight line. A dotted marquee defines the selected area.

Polygon Lasso tool

The Polygon Lasso tool creates a freeform selection with straight line segments.

1 Select the Polygon Lasso tool. Position your cursor on the image, then click; move the cursor, then click... and so on, until you have defined the area you want to select. Click back at the start point to complete the selection. Alternatively, you can double-click to close the selection marquee.

The Magnetic Lasso tool

The Magnetic Lasso tool is most useful when you want to select an object or an area of the image which contrasts strongly with the area surrounding it.

1 Select the Magnetic Lasso tool. Click on the edge of the object you want to select to place the first fastening point.

Hot tip

Hold down Shift, then click and drag around an area to add it to the selection. Hold down Alt/option, then click and drag around an area to remove it from the selection.

Hot tip

When you return to the start point with the Polygon Lasso tool, a small circle appears at the bottom right of the cursor to indicate that you can close the selection by clicking once.

Beware

You cannot use the Magnetic Lasso tool in 32-bit per channel images.

...cont'd

Either, move the cursor along the edge of the object, or click and drag along the edge to draw a freehand segment. As you move along the edge of the object, the "active" segment of the selection border snaps to the most clearly defined edge in the image near the cursor. Fastening points are added automatically, at intervals, as you drag.

2 To close the selection border, position your cursor on the start point, (a small circle at the cursor indicates that you are on the start point) then click. Alternatively, double-click, or press the Enter/Return key. Photoshop creates a segment from the point you have reached to the start point of the selection border. To close the selection border with a straight line segment, hold down Alt/option and double-click.

Lasso Width
The Magnetic Lasso tool detects edges within the specified distance from the cursor. Enter a value between 1–256 pixels.

Frequency
This setting determines the rate at which fastening points are set. Enter a value between 0–100. Set higher values to place fastening points at more frequent intervals.

Edge Contrast
Enter a value between 1–100%. This value determines how sensitive the Magnetic Lasso tool is to edges in the image. Higher values select edges that contrast strongly with their background. Lower values select edges that have smaller amounts of contrast.

The Magic Wand Tool

The Magic Wand tool selects continuous areas of color in an image, based on a tolerance setting. Low tolerance settings create a very limited selection of color. Higher settings select a wider range of pixels. The tool is good for selecting areas of reasonably consistent color.

Hot tip

To add to a selection using the Magic Wand tool, hold down Shift, then click on an unselected part of the image.

1 Before creating a selection using the Magic Wand tool, check the Tolerance setting. Enter a Tolerance value from 0–255. If you set a tolerance value of 255, you will select every pixel in the image.

2 Click on the image to select pixels of similar color value. All adjacent pixels that are within the Tolerance range are selected. Adjust the default setting of 32 as necessary to make the selection you require.

Hot tip

Typically, you refine Magic Wand selections using a combination of the other selection tools, together with the Grow, Similar and Refine Edge commands.

103

3 Deselect the Contiguous option to select pixels throughout the image that fall within the Tolerance setting. The result is similar to using the Similar command (see page 108.)

4 To deselect a selection marquee when the Magic Wand tool is selected, click inside the selection marquee. If you click outside the selection marquee, you create another selection based around the pixel where you clicked.

Beware

You cannot use the Magic Wand tool in Bitmap mode.

5 Use the Refine Edge command to evaluate and fine-tune your selection. (See page 105 for further information.)

The Quick Selection Tool

Hot tip

You can also click with the Quick Selection tool instead of dragging. This can sometimes make a more precise selection.

Using the Quick Selection tool is one of the quickest and easiest ways to select areas of pixels and objects with defined edges.

1 Click once on the Quick Selection tool to select it. Use the Brush Picker pop-up in the Options bar to set the size of the brush. (See page 76 for further information on setting brush options.)

2 Click and drag across an area of the image you want to select. The tool samples color in the area and then forms a selection of pixels which expands outward to defined contrast edges in the image.

Hot tip

If you use either the Add to Selection or Subtract from Selection option in the Options bar, remember to click back on the New Selection button to reset the tool to its default behavior.

3 After you create an initial selection with the Quick Selection tool, the Add to Selection option in the Options bar is selected automatically. Click and drag in the image to add further areas to the selection.

4 Select the Subtract from Selection button in the Options bar, then either click or click and drag in the existing selection to remove areas from the selection.

Hot tip

When using either the Add to Selection or Subtract from Selection tool, hold down Alt/option to switch temporarily between the two tools.

Sample All Layers – select this option if you want the selection to include pixels from other layers, not just the active layer.

Auto Enhance – select this option to create a more accurate, refined selection. Using this option Photoshop takes slightly longer to evaluate color values and form the selection.

Refine Edge

After you make a selection with any of the selection tools, you can evaluate and refine the selection edge using the Refine Edge command.

1 To refine a selection, with the selection tool still selected, click the Refine Edge button in the Options bar, or choose Select>Refine Edge.

2 Create settings using the Radius, Contrast, Smooth, Feather and Contract/Expand sliders to refine the selection.

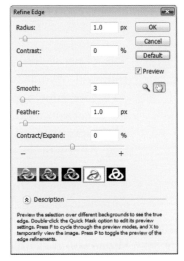

Hot tip

The Zoom and Hand tools are available in the Refine Edge dialog box so that you can move to different parts of the image and zoom in or out to assess the effect on the selection edge as you make changes to settings.

Radius – for areas of fine detail, the radius amount can help create a soft transition along the selection edge.

Contrast – can remove artifacts (unwanted detail) and make a selection sharper and crisper.

Smooth – helps smooth jagged edges in a selection, but can sometimes blur fine detail.

Feather – creates a soft-edged selection by blurring it.

Contract/Expand – decreases or increases the overall size of the selection.

3 Use the Selection Preview icons (Standard, Quick Mask, On Black, On White, Grayscale Mask) to evaluate the results of settings against a variety of different backgrounds. Using different previews helps you to assess settings effectively.

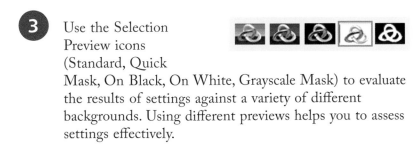

Hot tip

Whilst using the refine Edges dialog box, type F on the keyboard to cycle through the previews. Type X on the keyboard to toggle between the image and the preview method selected in the dialog box.

4 Click OK to apply settings to the image.

Feathering Selections

You can use the Feather option to control the degree to which the edge of a selection is softened or faded. Feathering a selection creates a transition boundary between the selection and the surrounding pixels, which can cause a loss of detail.

1 Select one of the Lasso tools, or the Rectangular or Elliptical Marquee selection tool. In the Options bar, set a Feather value, e.g. 10. The amount you set depends on the effect you want to achieve. Use higher values on high resolution images. Create a selection using a selection tool. Alternatively, using any of the selection tools, you can make a selection and then choose Select>Refine Edge. Enter a value in the Feather entry box, or drag the slider.

2 When you move the selection, using the Move tool, you will see the feathered edge around the selection and also where you move the selection from.

Creating a vignette

You can use the feathering option to create a vignette, or soft, fading edge to an image.

1 Set a Feather value in the Options bar for the selection tool you are using. Next, create a selection, which can be a regular or irregular shape. Choose Select>Inverse. This reverses the selection – selecting all the pixels that were previously not selected. Press Delete (Mac) or Backspace (Windows) to delete the area surrounding your selection, leaving a feathered edge.

Modifying Selections

There are many instances when you need to add to or subtract from a selection. You can use any combination of selection tools to make the selection you want. For example, you might start by making a selection with the Magic Wand tool, then add to the selection using the Lasso tool.

1. To add to an existing selection, hold down the Shift key, then click and drag to create another selection marquee that intersects the existing selection marquee.

2. You can use the same technique to create non-adjoining selections. Although the selections may be in different parts of the image, they count and act as one selection. For example, if you apply a filter, the effect will be apparent in all the selection marquees.

3. To add to a selection, hold down Shift and use the Lasso tool to quickly loop around small areas that the Magic Wand tool typically misses out from its selection.

4. To subtract from a selection, hold down Alt/option, then click and drag with a selection tool to intersect the existing selection marquee. The area defined by the intersecting marquee is removed from the original selection.

Hot tip

To modify an existing selection, select a Selection tool, then click the Add to ... , Subtract from ... , or Intersect with Selection button in the Options bar. These settings remain in effect for the tool.

It's worth reselecting the New Selection button, so that previous selections do not cause unexpected results the next time you use the tool.

Hot tip

For complex selections, it can be quite useful to hide the dotted selection border temporarily, in order to see the selected pixels more clearly. Choose View>Show>Selection Edges to hide the selection border. The selection remains active; you have simply hidden the border. Choose the same option to redisplay the selection border.

Grow and Similar Commands

The Grow and Similar commands are very useful when used in conjunction with the Magic Wand tool to add to a selection. Both work according to the Tolerance value set in the Magic Wand Options bar.

The Grow command selects contiguous or adjoining areas of color based on the Tolerance setting in the Magic Wand Options bar.

1 Make a selection. Check that the Tolerance setting in the Magic Wand Options bar is appropriate.

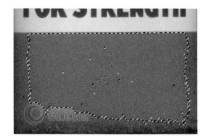

2 Choose Select>Grow to add pixels to the existing selection which fall within the Tolerance setting and are adjacent to pixels already in the selection.

The Similar command selects non-adjacent pixels that fall within the same Tolerance setting as set in the Magic Wand Options bar.

1 Make a selection using any of the selection tools. Check that the Tolerance setting in the Magic Wand Options bar is appropriate.

2 Choose Select>Similar to select pixels throughout the image that fall within the Tolerance setting.

Pasting Into Selections

Pasting into selections is useful for compositing images.

1 Create a selection in the destination window.

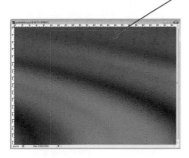 

2 Open the source document, then make the selection you want to paste into the destination document. Choose Edit>Copy to copy the selection to the Clipboard.

3 Click in the destination image window. The selection should still be active. Choose Edit>Paste Into (Ctrl/Command+ Shift+V) to paste the Clipboard selection into the selected area.

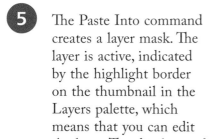

4 Use the Move tool to reposition the pasted selection relative to the original selection.

5 The Paste Into command creates a layer mask. The layer is active, indicated by the highlight border on the thumbnail in the Layers palette, which means that you can edit the layer. To edit the mask, click the Mask icon in the Layers palette. The highlight border appears on the mask to indicate that the layer mask is selected.

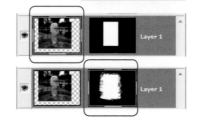

Beware

When you paste into a selection, the selection from the Clipboard is rendered at the resolution of the destination document. This means that the selection copied from the source document changes size if the resolution of the two documents is different.

Hot tip

Make sure the layer mask is selected, then paint with black to add to the mask, or paint with white to subtract from it. (See pages 166–167, "Layer Masks".)

Filling a Selection

You can use the Fill dialog box in order to fill an entire layer or a selection.

See pages 81–83 for a description of the blending modes.

1 To fill a selection, first define either a foreground or background color that you want to fill with, then make a selection. Choose Edit>Fill. Use the Use pop-up to choose the fill type. You can also set Opacity for the fill and a Blending Mode. Click OK.

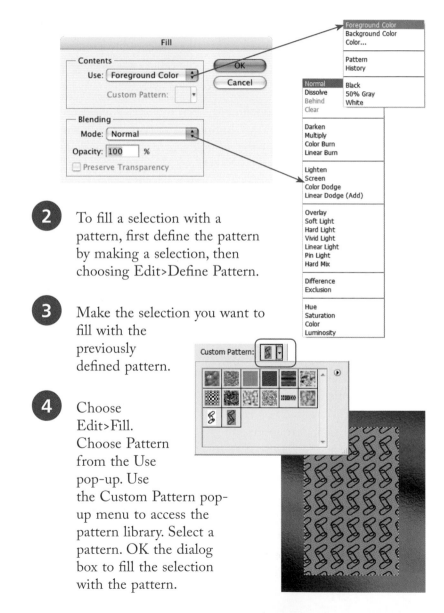

2 To fill a selection with a pattern, first define the pattern by making a selection, then choosing Edit>Define Pattern.

Beware

If you don't make a selection before you choose the Fill command, you fill the entire layer.

3 Make the selection you want to fill with the previously defined pattern.

4 Choose Edit>Fill. Choose Pattern from the Use pop-up. Use the Custom Pattern pop-up menu to access the pattern library. Select a pattern. OK the dialog box to fill the selection with the pattern.

Copying and Pasting Selections

You can use the Clipboard to copy and paste selections within the same image and into other images. You can also drag selections between images.

1 To copy a selection, first make a selection using any of the selection tools. Choose Edit>Copy.

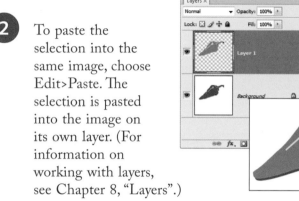

2 To paste the selection into the same image, choose Edit>Paste. The selection is pasted into the image on its own layer. (For information on working with layers, see Chapter 8, "Layers".)

3 To paste the selection into another image that is already open, click on the other image window to make it active. Choose Edit>Paste to paste the selection from the Clipboard onto a new layer in the active image.

4 You can also drag a selection from one image window into another. You need two image windows open – the source and the destination windows. Make a selection in the source window, select the Move tool, position your cursor within the selection, then click and drag into the destination window. The selection appears on its own layer.

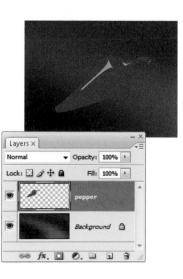

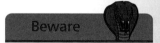

Hot tip

A useful technique for selecting a simple image, like the pepper on this page, is the Inverse selection command. Use the Magic Wand tool to select the background, then choose Select>Inverse to reverse the selection. The areas that represent the pepper are now selected.

Beware

In this example the pepper is filled with 50% gray and offset slightly from its original position when pasted to make the copy obvious in the screenshot.

Transforming Selections

The ability to transform a selection's bounding box enables you to fine tune selections, distort selections and make selections that were previously difficult to achieve.

Beware

The Transform Selection bounding box transforms the selection border only. It does not transform the pixels within the selection.

1 To transform a selection, choose Select>Transform Selection. A bounding box with eight handles appears around the selection. A Reference Point marker appears at the center of the bounding box.

2 To scale a selection, click and drag a handle. The cursor becomes a bi-directional arrow. To scale a selection in proportion, hold down Shift then drag a handle.

Hot tip

Drag the Reference Point marker ( ) to a new location to specify the point around which transformations take place.

112

3 To rotate a selection, position your cursor just outside the selection border. The cursor changes to a bi-directional, curved arrow. Click and drag in a circular direction.

4 To distort the selection boundary, hold down Ctrl/Command then drag a corner handle.

5 To create a perspective effect on the selection border, hold down Ctrl/Command+Alt/option+Shift, then drag a corner handle.

Hot tip

Press the Enter key on the keyboard to commit or accept a transformation. Press the Esc key to abandon changes. You can also double-click inside the transform bounding box to accept a transformation.

6 To shear a selection border, hold down Ctrl/Command, then click and drag a center top/bottom or center left/right handle.

7 Click the Cancel button in the Options bar to reject changes. Click the Commit button to apply the transformation.

8 Layers

Layers introduce considerable flexibility into the way you can work with images. Layers let you keep various image elements separate so that you can make changes to the pixels on one layer without affecting pixels on another. Additional layers increase the file size of the image. When you finish editing your image, you can flatten the image to merge all layers into a single Background layer.

Working with Layers

When you create or open an image for the first time, it consists of one default layer called Background.

Beware

New layers are created automatically when you use the Type tool to add text to an image, when you drag or copy a selection into an image, and also when you drag a layer from one document into another.

1 To create a new layer, choose New Layer from the palette menu ( ). Enter a name for the new layer in the name entry box. You can also choose Opacity and Blending Mode settings at this stage if required.

Hot tip

After you create a layer, choose Layer Properties from the palette menu if you need to edit layer options for the layer.

2 Alternatively, click once on the New Layer icon at the bottom of the Layers palette to create a new layer with default settings. Hold down Alt/option, then click the New Layer icon to access the New Layer dialog box.

3 OK the dialog box. This creates a new, empty layer, which appears in the Layers palette above the previously active layer. Notice also that the file size in the Document Sizes status bar area increases when you paint on or add pixels to the layer.

114

Hot tip

One of the most useful techniques for creating a new layer is to make a selection on a part of the Background layer, then choose Layer>New>Layer via Copy (Ctrl/Command+J). The selection of pixels is copied to a new layer. You can now edit and transform the pixels on the new layer with the original pixels intact on the Background layer.

4 To name a layer, position your cursor on the layer's label, then double-click. Enter a new name in the label entry area, then press Enter/Return on the keyboard.

5 To delete the active layer, choose Delete Layer from the palette menu. Click Yes or No in the delete warning box. Or, drag the Layer name onto the Wastebasket icon at the bottom of the Layers palette. No warning alert appears if you use this method.

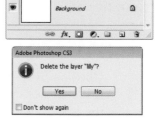

Selecting, hiding and showing layers

You can only paint, edit pixels or make color adjustments to one layer at a time. This is often referred to as the "target" or active layer.

1 Click on the layer name in the Layers palette to make it active. The layer name highlights to indicate that it is active. The name of the active layer appears in the title bar of the image window.

lilly-layers-start.psd @ 40% (lilly, RGB/8)

2 To hide the contents of a layer, click on the Eye icon in the leftmost column of the Layers palette. To show a layer, click in the leftmost column to bring back the Eye icon.

Reordering layers

You cannot change the stacking order of the Background layer, but it is often necessary to change the stacking order of other layers to control which layers appear in front of other layers.

1 To change the layer order, click and drag the layer name you want to reposition. Notice the horizontal bar that appears as you move the layer upwards or downwards. Release the mouse when the horizontal bar appears in the position to which you want the layer moved.

Repositioning layer contents

You can reposition the entire contents of a layer using the Move tool.

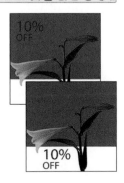

1 Click on the layer you want to move in the Layers palette. Select the Move tool, then position your cursor anywhere on the image. Click and drag to move the layer.

Hot tip

Click the Eye icon to hide/show a layer group and also a layer style.

Hot tip

To select all pixels on a layer, hold down Ctrl/ Command and click on the layer name in the Layers palette.

Hot tip

You can nudge the contents of a selected layer in 1-pixel increments by pressing the arrow keys when the Move tool is selected.

115

Merge and Flatten Layers

Use the Merge commands to combine two or more layers into one layer. This is useful for keeping the file size down and for consolidating elements on different layers into a single manageable layer or unit.

1 To merge all the visible layers in your document, first hide any layers you don't want to merge. Make sure one of the layers you want to merge is active, then choose Merge Visible from the palette menu (⚏), or choose Layer>Merge Visible.

116

2 To merge a layer with the layer below it, first select the layer, then choose Merge Down from the palette menu, or choose Layer>Merge Down.

Flattening images

When you flatten an image, you end up with a Background layer only. This reduces the file size. Flatten an image when you have finished creating and positioning the elements of your composite image, and are ready to save the file in a suitable format for placing in a page layout application.

1 To flatten an image, make sure that all the layers you want to keep are visible. Choose Flatten Image from the Layers palette menu, or choose Layers>Flatten Image.

Moving Layers Between Images

You can copy a complete layer from one Photoshop document to another, similar to the way you move a selection from one document to another.

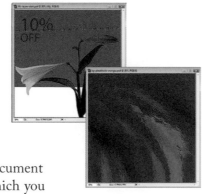

1. First make sure you have two document windows open – a "source" document and a "destination" document. The source document contains the layer you want to copy. The destination document is the document into which you want to copy the layer.

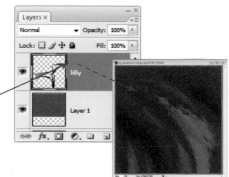

2. Click in the source document window to make it active. Position your cursor on the layer in the Layers palette, then drag the layer you want to copy from the source document into the destination document window. A bounding box indicates the layer you are copying.

3. Position the layer and then release the mouse. The layer is positioned above the previously active layer in the destination document's Layers palette. The destination document becomes the active image window.

Beware

The layer you move into the destination image window is rendered at the resolution of that window. This may cause the elements on the moved layer to appear larger or smaller than in the original window. To avoid surprises, make sure that the source and destination images are at the same resolution. Also, if the modes of the two images are different, the layer you move is converted to match the mode of the destination window.

Don't forget

If necessary, use the Defringe command (Layer>Matting>Defringe) to remove any fringe around pixels on a layer that you copy from one image to another.

Selecting and Linking Layers

Selecting multiple layers creates a temporary grouping that allows you to manipulate two or more layers as a unit. Linking layers keeps the layers grouped until you unlink them. You can move, align and transform multiple selected layers or linked layers, and also apply styles from the Styles palette.

1 To select multiple, consecutive layers, select the first layer, hold down Shift, then click the last layer in the range. To select multiple, non-consecutive layers, select the first layer, hold down Ctrl/Command, then click each layer you want to add to the selection.

2 To remove a multiple selection of layers, click on any individual layer in the Layers palette. Or, click in an empty area below the bottom-most layer in the palette.

3 To link layers, select two or more consecutive, or non-consecutive layers. Then click the Link button () at the bottom of the Layers palette. A link icon appears to the right of a linked layer. When you select a linked layer in the Layers palette, all other layers linked to it display a link icon to indicate their linked status.

4 To unlink a single layer, select the specific layer you want to unlink, then click the Link button. Other layers in a set of linked layers remain linked.

5 To unlink all layers in a link set, either select each link manually, or select one linked layer, then choose Layer>Select Linked Layers. Click the Link button to unlink all linked layers.

Locking Layers

There are four levels of lock that can be applied to layers. A dimmed lock icon appears to the right of the layer when you select one of the lock options. A solid lock icon appears when the layer is fully locked. The Background layer is fully locked by default.

Don't forget

Transparent areas on a layer are indicated by the checkerboard pattern when the Background layer is hidden.

1 To completely lock a layer, select the layer in the Layers palette, then click the Lock All option.

You will not be able to reposition the layer or make any changes to it, including changing blending mode, opacity and layer style.

2 To prevent the layer from being moved using the Move tool, click the Lock Position option.

Hot tip

You can move locked layers to a new position in the stacking order of layers, but you cannot delete a fully locked layer.

3 To disable painting tools on the layer, select the Lock Image pixels option.

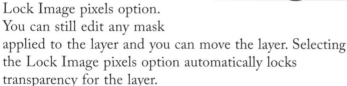

You can still edit any mask applied to the layer and you can move the layer. Selecting the Lock Image pixels option automatically locks transparency for the layer.

4 Click Lock Transparency to preserve transparent areas of a layer. You can make changes to

the existing pixels on the layer, but you cannot make changes to any areas of transparency. For example, if Lock Transparency is selected, the blur filters do not work effectively on the layer as pixels cannot spread into the areas of transparency to create the blur effect.

Hot tip

The Lock Transparency and Lock Image Pixels options are automatically selected for Type layers. You cannot turn these options off.

Adjustment Layers

Don't forget

An adjustment layer is created above the currently active layer. It's settings apply to the layers below it and do not affect layers above.

Using an adjustment layer is like positioning a lens above the pixels on the layers below it to change their appearance. If you don't like the result, you can edit the adjustment layer to achieve the result you want, or you can discard it. When you are satisfied with the result you can implement the adjustment layer as a permanent change.

1 Select a layer in the Layers palette. The adjustment layer is created above the currently active layer. Choose Layer>New Adjustment Layer. Choose a type from the New Adjustment Layer sub-menu. This automatically becomes the name for the layer. In the New Layer dialog box, enter a different name if desired. Set Opacity and Blending Mode at this stage if you want to. Click OK.

Hot tip

You can copy and paste adjustment layers between images in order to apply consistent color and tonal changes to different images.

2 As an alternative, you can click the New Adjustment Layer button ( ) at the bottom of the Layers palette, then choose an adjustment layer type.

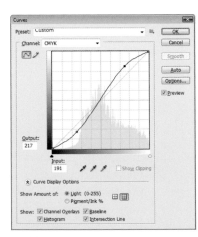

Hot tip

By reducing the Opacity setting for an adjustment layer you can lessen the effect of the settings you create in the adjustment layer dialog box.

3 Depending on the type of adjustment layer you chose, the appropriate dialog box opens. Create the settings you want to apply. OK the dialog box.

4 The new adjustment layer appears in the Layers palette as the active layer. The settings you create now apply to all layers below the adjustment layer.

Create a selection before you create an adjustment layer to limit the effects of the adjustment layer settings to a specific area of an image:

5 Click the Eye icon to hide/show the preview of the changes brought about by the adjustment layer settings. Double-click the adjustment layer to re-enter the appropriate adjustment dialog box to make changes to the settings.

6 Drag the adjustment layer into the Wastebasket if you want to discard the settings.

7 When you are ready to make the settings of the adjustment layer permanent, either use one of the Merge commands from the palette menu, or flatten the image.

The adjustment layer settings do not have a permanent effect on pixels until the layer is merged with other layers, or the image is flattened.

Layer Groups

When you create complex images with multiple layers it is convenient to simplify the layers palette by combining related layers together into a layer group. Creating layer groups in complex, multi-layered images makes it much easier to manage the elements in the image.

Hot tip

In the New Group from Layers dialog box, leave the Mode option set to Pass Through to ensure that blending and opacity settings apply to all layers in an image and are not limited to the layers in the layer set.

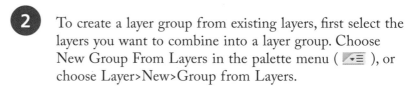

1 To create a new layer group, click the Create New Group button ( ) in the bottom of the Layers palette to use the current default settings, or choose New Group from the palette menu.

2 To create a layer group from existing layers, first select the layers you want to combine into a layer group. Choose New Group From Layers in the palette menu ( ), or choose Layer>New>Group from Layers.

Hot tip

To nest a layer group within another layer group, drag the layer group you want to nest onto an existing layer group folder.

3 To move a layer into a layer group, drag it onto the layer group folder. Release the mouse when the layer group folder highlights. The layer is positioned at the bottom of the layers already in the layer group. If the layer group is expanded, drag the layer to the desired position. Release when the highlight bar is in the correct position.

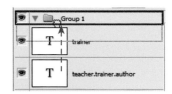

4 Click the Collapse/ Expand triangle to reveal or hide the layers contained within the layer group.

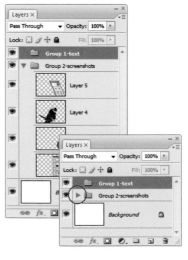

Layer Styles

Use the Layer Style sub-menu, to create sophisticated layer effects such as soft shadows, beveled and embossed edges, and inner and outer glows quickly and easily. This example consists of 3 layers – a white Background layer, a colored circle Shape layer and a colored triangle Shape layer, and uses Bevel and Emboss options to demonstrate the principles for creating a layer style.

1 To apply a layer style, click on a layer in the Layers palette to make it active. Choose Layer>Layer Style>Bevel & Emboss. In the Structure section, choose a style from the Style pop-up menu and a technique from the Technique pop-up menu. Select the Up/Down radio button to light the effect from above or below.

2 Use the Depth entry box or slider to adjust the height of the effect. Use the Size slider to control the spread of the bevel. The Soften slider controls the overall intensity of the effect and helps reduce irregularities or artifacts in the effect, creating a smoother result.

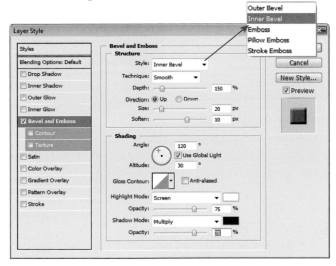

3 In the Shading area, enter a value in the Angle entry box to control the direction of the light source. Enter a value in the Altitude entry box to define the apparent depth of the light source. Drag in the Angle/Altitude disk to create settings manually if you prefer.

Hot tip

You can also select a layer style option using the Add Layer Style button at the bottom of the Layers palette:

Don't forget

Each layer style provides a range of options specific to that style. Experiment with the options to achieve the effect you want.

Hot tip

In the Layer Style dialog box, make sure the Preview option is selected to see the effect applied in the image.

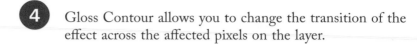

...cont'd

You cannot apply a layer style to the Background layer, a layer set or a locked layer.

4 Gloss Contour allows you to change the transition of the effect across the affected pixels on the layer.

5 Adjust settings for the Highlight and Shadow edges of the effect. It is a good idea initially to leave the blending modes set to Screen and Multiply respectively. Experiment with the Opacity sliders to create a more subtle effect.

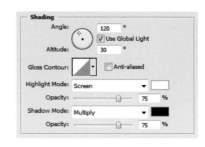

Click on the Expand/ Collapse triangle to hide or show the layer styles applied to a layer:

6 OK the dialog when you are satisfied with the results. Notice in the Layers palette a *fx* symbol on the layer, indicating that there is a layer effect applied to the layer. Whilst the *fx* symbol appears the layer effect remains editable.

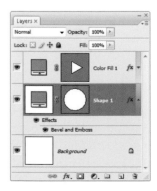

Managing Layer Styles

Once you have created a layer style you can continue to edit the effect and you can use a variety of commands from the Layer Style sub-menu to manage the effects.

Click the eye icon to the left of the layer effect to control its visibility:

1 To edit layer style settings, select the layer, then click the Expand triangle to display layer effects as separate entries in the Layers palette. Double-click the name of the effect you want to edit. You can adjust settings as often as you need to achieve the desired result.

...cont'd

2 To keep the angle of
the light source constant
if you are using layer
effects on more than one
layer in an image, choose
Layer>Layer Style>

Global Light. Enter a value for the Angle in the Angle
entry box. OK the dialog box. Make sure you select the
Use Global Light checkbox in the Layer Style dialog box
when you create multiple layer effects.

3 To copy exact layer style settings from
one layer to another, first select a
layer with a layer effect applied to it,
then choose Copy Layer Style from
the Layer Style sub-menu. Click on
another layer in the Layers palette.
Choose Paste Layer Style from the
Layer Style sub-menu.

4 To permanently remove layer styles
from a layer, make sure you
select the appropriate layer,
then choose Layer>Layer
Style>Clear Layer Styles.

5 Layer styles automate
procedures that in the
past you had to perform
yourself. Use the Create
Layer command from
the Layer Styles sub-
menu to separate the
layer effect into the
multiple layers that
Photoshop uses to
create the effect. This
can be useful if you
need to edit specific
parts of the effect.

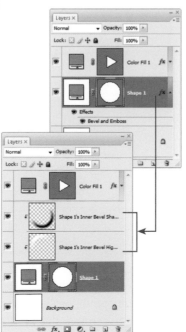

Hot tip

To temporarily disable
layer effects on all layers,
not just the active layer,
choose Layer>Layer
Style>Hide All Effects.
Choose Layer>Layer
Style>Show All Effects to
reverse the process.

Beware

Once you merge a
layer with a layer effect
applied to it, you can no
longer adjust the layer
effect settings.

125

Transforming Layers

Once you have moved pixels to a new layer you can then transform the layer. Using Free Transform you can scale, rotate, distort, skew and create perspective effects.

1 Ensure the layer is active. Choose Edit>Free Transform. A bounding box with handles appears around the pixels. To scale a layer, drag a handle. To scale in proportion, hold down Shift then drag a corner handle.

2 To rotate a layer, position your cursor slightly outside the bounding box. The cursor changes to a bi-directional arrow. Drag in a circular direction. You can drag the Reference Point marker to a new position to specify the point around which the rotation takes place.

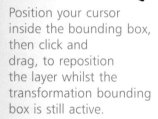

3 To skew the layer, hold down Ctrl/Command+Shift, then drag the center top/bottom, or the center left/right handle.

4 To create perspective, hold down Ctrl/Command+Alt/option+Shift then drag a corner handle. To distort the layer, hold down Ctrl/Command then drag a corner handle. This allows you to move corner handles independently.

5 Click the Cancel button in the Options bar, or press Esc to revert to the original state without making changes. Click the Commit button or press Return/Enter to accept the transformation and remove the Transformation bounding box.

New Layer Commands

The New Layer via Cut (Ctrl/Command+Shift+J) and the New Layer via Copy (Ctrl/Command+J) commands are essential options when creating layers. Use these commands to either cut or copy selected pixels to a new layer.

1 Start by making a selection. Then choose Layer>New>Layer via Copy to create a new layer containing a copy of the selected pixels. The new layer is automatically named Layer 1, etc, depending on the number of layers already in the document. The new layer is created above the layer that is active when you choose the Layer via Copy command.

2 Make a selection, then choose New Layer via Cut to cut the selected pixels to a new layer. Notice when you reposition the pixels on the new layer, the area on the Background layer from which they were cut is filled with the current background color.

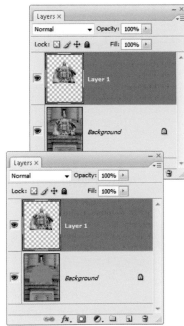

Layer Comps

A layer comp is a snapshot of an image that records the visibility and position of layers, and any layer styles for an image at a particular point in time. Layer comps provide a convenient means for recording various permutations of image layers without having to create multiple, separate image files. Unlike Snapshots created in the History palette, Layer comps are saved with the file.

1 Click the Layer Comps button, or choose Window>Layer Comps to show the Layer Comps palette.

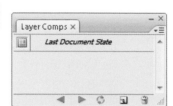

2 Create the arrangement and visibility settings for the layer palette that you want to record, then either click the Create New Layer Comp button () at the bottom of the palette, or choose New Layer Comp from the palette menu.

3 In the New Layer Comp dialog box, enter a name for the Layer Comp. Select Visibility, Position and Appearance options that you want to record in the Layer Comp.

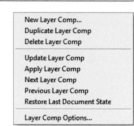

4 Add an additional explanatory note in the Comment entry box if required.

5 Click OK. The New Layer Comp is added at the bottom of the Layer Comps palette, below any existing Layer Comps.

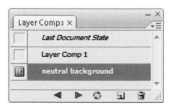

Managing Layer Comps

Layer Comps add flexibility and a degree of complexity to the way in which you work with and manage images. You should be careful about the way you manage layer comp variations in order to work effectively, smoothly and productively.

1 To change the name of a layer comp, double-click the layer comp name in the Layer Comp palette to highlight the existing name. Enter a new name then press Return/Enter.

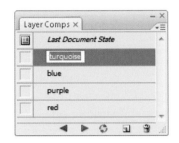

2 To change the layer comp settings you selected when you first created the layer comp, double-click the layer comp entry line (but not directly on the layer comp name) to access the Layer Comp Options dialog box. Make changes as required.

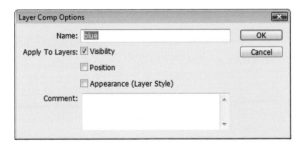

3 To display a layer comp in the image window, either click in the Apply Layer Comp box to the left of the layer comp name, or click the Apply Previous/ Next Selected Layer Comp arrow button at the bottom of the palette.

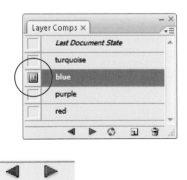

129

...cont'd

4 Click the Apply Last Document State box, or choose Restore Last Document State from the palette menu to return to the state of the document you are currently working on.

Hot tip

Layer Comps add to the file size of an image. It is a good idea to delete at least some of your layer comps when they are no longer required.

5 If you make changes to a layer, for example, deleting a layer that is already recorded as an element in a Layer Comp, a warning triangle appears to the right of all layer comps that are affected. You can update the layer comp with the new settings by selecting the layer comp, then clicking the Update Layer Comp button ( ), or choosing Update Layer Comp from the palette menu.

6 To delete a layer comp, click on it to select it, then click the Wastebasket icon at the bottom of the palette, or drag the layer comp into the Wastebasket. There is no warning message when you delete a layer comp. Use the History palette if necessary to restore a deleted layer comp.

Smart Objects

Smart Objects provide enhanced flexibility as you work in Photoshop as they can be edited outside the parent file as independent components. Also, you can make repeated edits and transformations to Smart Objects without degrading image quality. You can import vector Smart Objects from Adobe Illustrator, or you can create Smart Objects from selected layers within Photoshop.

Vector Smart Objects from Illustrator

Pasting or placing Illustrator artwork as a vector Smart Object allows you to make multiple, non-destructive changes to the artwork in Photoshop. Photoshop achieves this by retaining a link to the original Illustrator artwork which it then continues to reference as you edit and transform it.

1 Working in Illustrator, select the artwork you want to use as a Smart Object in Photoshop. Choose Edit>Copy to copy the artwork to the clipboard.

2 In a Photoshop file, choose Edit>Paste. In the Paste dialog box select the Smart Object radio button. Click OK.

3 The Illustrator artwork appears in a bounding box in the center of the screen area. Position your cursor inside the bounding box, then click and drag to reposition the object if necessary. Drag bounding box handles to scale the artwork to the required size. Hold down Shift, then drag a corner handle to scale the object in proportion.

4 Click the Commit button in the options bar when you are ready to place the object on a new layer as a Smart Object. Or, press enter on the keyboard. The object

Hot tip

Working with Smart Objects externally to the parent document can make it easier to edit specific elements within a complex Photoshop project.

131

Don't forget

Think of Smart Objects as child elements, or embedded files, that exist within the main parent Photoshop document.

Hot tip

Double-clicking a Vector Smart Object layer launches Illustrator if it is not already running.

...cont'd

Beware

You must keep the Illustrator file in the same folder location and with the same name for Photoshop to work with it as a Smart Object.

Beware

You cannot apply Perspective, Distort or Warp transformations to Smart Objects.

creates a Vector Smart Object layer. The Smart Object icon appears in the layer thumbnail in the Layers palette to indicate that it is a Smart Object layer.

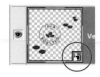

5 To edit the original Smart Object element in Illustrator either double-click the Vector Smart Object thumbnail, or, make sure the layer is active then choose Edit Contents from the Layers palette menu. A warning dialog box reminds you to save any changes you make in Illustrator so that the Photoshop document updates accordingly when you return to it.

Smart Objects from Photoshop Layers

1 To create a Smart Object from existing Photoshop layers, first select one or more layers. Choose Convert to Smart Object from the Layers palette menu. The selected layers convert to a single Smart Object layer.

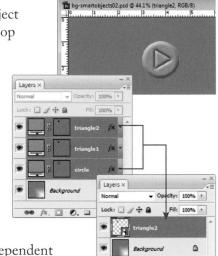

2 To edit the Smart Object layer as an independent file, double-click the Smart Object layer thumbnail. A warning message reminds you to choose File>Save to commit any changes you make to the external Smart Object.

3 To return to the parent Photoshop document and update it with changes made to the Smart Object externally, close the Smart Object window. Click save if prompted.

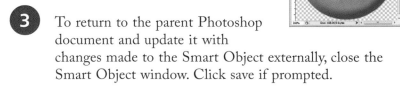

Warping

Warping is a type of transformation that allows you to bend objects on layers to create interesting effects, or to map objects to curved surfaces. You can create custom warp effects manually, or you can choose from a variety of warp styles which you can then customize to meet your requirements.

Hot tip

You cannot apply Warp transformations to Vector Smart Object layers.

1 To warp a selected layer, choose Edit>Transform>Warp. A default warp mesh appears on the contents of the layer.

2 To manually create a custom warp effect, you can drag any of the warp gridlines, drag within any of the mesh segments, or you can drag any of the corner anchor points, or direction points that appear around the edge of the warp mesh. These direction points function in the same way as direction points on a curve segment of a path (see Chapter 10, "Paths" for further details).

Hot tip

You can use Edit>Undo to undo the last custom warp adjustment.

Using Warp presets

1 To warp a selected layer using a preset style, choose Edit>Transform>Warp.

2 Select a warp preset from the Warp style pop-up menu.

None
✔ Custom
Arc
Arc Lower
Arc Upper
Arch
Bulge
Shell Lower
Shell Upper
Flag
Wave
Fish
Rise
Fisheye
Inflate
Squeeze
Twist

...cont'd

3 To customize the preset warp style, either drag the Bend anchor point which appears on the warp mesh, or enter a value in the Bend entry box in the Options bar.

4 In the Options bar you can enter values in the H entry box (-100–100) to apply horizontal distortion. Enter a value in the V entry box (-100–100) to apply vertical distortion.

5 Click the Change Warp Orientation button in the Options bar to apply the warp from the opposite orientation.

Click the Switch Warp button in the Options bar to switch from a warp mesh to a standard free transform bounding box or vice versa:

Auto-Align/Blend Layers

Auto-Align Layers and Auto-Blend layers work with content on different layers in an image. To use the Auto-Align/Blend commands, select two or more layers in the layers palette.

Auto-Align Layers

Auto-Align aligns layers based on similarities in image content on layers. It can be used to create panoramic effects, or to align layers with similar content so that you can create a composite image by painting in preferred content from another aligned layer.

1 To align two or more selected layers, choose Edit>Auto-Align Layers. Select a Projection option in the Auto-Align Layers dialog box.

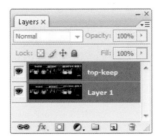

Auto – based on an analysis of the layers uses Perspective or Cylindrical to produce the best result.

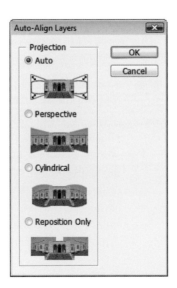

Perspective – useful for panoramic effects where there is overlapping detail in the image content of the layers. The central image is typically used as a reference. It applies skew and stretch transformations on layers if necessary.

Cylindrical – useful for extensive panoramas. Overlapping content is matched. The central image is typically used as a reference.

Reposition Only – matches similarities in content, but without skewing or stretching layer content.

2 For panoramic effects, use the Auto-Blend Layers command (see next section).

...cont'd

3 To create a composite image from aligned layers, create a layer mask on the topmost layer. (See pages 166–167 for information on layer masks). With the layer mask selected, select the Paintbrush tool. Select a soft edge brush, then paint with black to hide pixels on the mask and allow pixels on the layer below to show through.

Auto-Blend Layers

Auto-Blend works by applying layer masks to layers and is useful for stitching together a panorama.

136

1 Use the Auto-Align Layers command to create a panorama by matching overlapping content for two or more selected layers. When you are satisfied with the alignment, choose Edit>Auto-Blend Layers. Photoshop creates layer masks for each layer as required to mask out areas where exposure may vary resulting in smooth transitions between image detail on individual layers.

The Styles Palette

When you want to apply layer style effects consistently and quickly it is easy to save layer styles in the Styles palette for later use. Photoshop ships with a wide variety of preset styles that you can use as the basis for experimentation.

Styles apply to layers – you cannot apply a style to the default Background layer.

You can apply styles to Type and Shape layers without having to rasterize them first.

Creating Styles

1 Click the Styles palette icon if the palette is in the palette dock, or choose Window>Styles to show the palette.

2 Create a layer style using the custom layer effects you want to include when you save the style. (See pages 123–125 for information on working with layer styles.) Make sure the layer remains active.

3 Choose New Style from the Styles palette menu ( ). Enter a name for the style in the New Style dialog box, then click OK. The new style appears in the Styles palette.

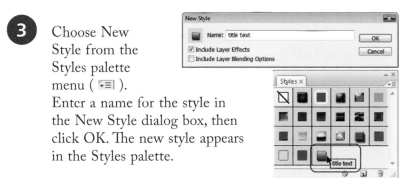

Applying Styles

1 In the Layers palette, select a layer to which you want to apply a style.

2 Click on a style in the Styles palette to apply it to the selected layer. To remove a style from a layer, click the No Style button ( ) in the Styles palette.

...cont'd

3 In the layers palette the ⨍𝑥 icon indicates a style applied to the layer. Click the expand triangle to show/hide the layer style effects applied to the layer.

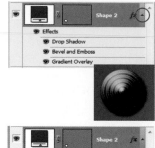

4 Click the Visibility button (👁) to hide or show individual layer effects, or all layer effects.

Editing Styles

1 To edit an individual layer effect, double-click the layer effect name in the layers palette. This takes you back into the Layer Style dialog

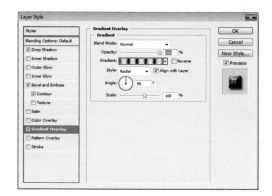

box which displays the settings currently in force. Adjust settings to create the effect you require. Make sure the Preview checkbox is selected to see the results of changes you make to settings reflected in the image.

Appending Styles

1 Use the Styles palette menu (▾☰) to load collections of preset styles that ship with Photoshop. Click the Append button to retain the default styles and add the selected collection to the palette.

Abstract Styles
Buttons
Dotted Strokes
Glass Buttons
Image Effects
Photographic Effects
Text Effects 2
Text Effects
Textures
Web Styles

Hot tip

Applying a preset style from the Styles palette, then examining and editing the settings used to create the overall effect is a really good way to build your understanding of the capabilities and potential offered by layer styles.

Hot tip

Choose Reset Styles from the Styles palette menu to return to the original default styles.

9 Working with Type

Type is not always an essential ingredient of an image, but when you need it, Photoshop offers a full range of powerful, sophisticated typesetting controls.

Creating Point Type

You can create two kinds of type: point type and paragraph type. Typically, you use point type when you want to work with small amounts of text, such as a single character, word, or line. Use paragraph type when you are working with more extensive blocks of type in paragraphs.

1 To create point type, select the Horizontal Type tool. You can create settings for the type using options in the Options bar, or the Character and Paragraph palettes, before you enter the type, or you can format the type after you enter it.

Hot tip

You can also commit type by pressing the Enter key on the numeric keypad, or selecting any other tool in the Toolbox.

2 Position your cursor in the image window, then click to place the text insertion point. Clicking with the Horizontal Type tool takes Photoshop into text editing mode.

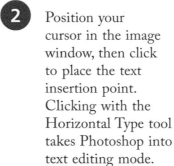

Point type

Don't forget

You must be in text editing mode to enter, edit or format text.

3 Enter text using the keyboard. You must press Enter (Windows), Return (Mac) on the main keyboard to begin a new line. Point type does not wrap.

4 Click on the Commit button in the Options bar when you have finished entering or editing type to commit the Type layer. This takes Photoshop out of text editing mode and you can now perform other tasks on the image. The type appears on its own layer. Click the Cancel button to discard the type.

Beware

For images in Multichannel, Bitmap or Indexed Color mode, type does not appear on its own layer, it appears as pixels on the Background layer and cannot be edited.

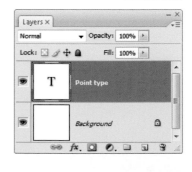

Creating Paragraph Type

When you work with Paragraph type, you define the width of the column of text. The text wraps to a new line when it reaches the edge of the type bounding box.

1 To create Paragraph type, select the Horizontal Type tool. You can create settings for the type using options in the Options bar, or the Character and Paragraph palettes before you enter the type, or you can format the type after you enter it.

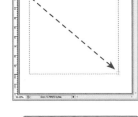

2 Position your cursor at one corner of the type area you want to create. Drag diagonally to define the size of the type's bounding box.

3 With the Horizontal Type tool selected, you can hold down Alt/ option, then click in the image to access the Paragraph Text Size dialog box. Enter values for Width and Height, then click OK.

4 Enter text using the keyboard. Text wraps when it reaches the edge of the type bounding box. Press Enter/Return on the main keyboard only when you want to begin a new paragraph.

> This is type that is entered in a bounding box created by dragging with the Horizontal Type tool. Type wraps when it reaches the edge of the bounding box.

5 Click on the Commit button in the Options bar to accept the Type layer. Or, click the Cancel button to abandon changes. Both buttons take Photoshop out of Text Editing mode and you can now perform other tasks on the image. The type appears on its own layer.

If you enter more type than can fit in the type bounding box, an overflow symbol appears in the bottom right corner of the bounding box:

> bounding box. The overset text marker appears in the bottom right corner handle to

Make the type smaller, or the box bigger, to see all the type.

Hot tip

To resize the type bounding box, select the Horizontal Type tool, click on the Type layer in the Layers palette, then click in the text itself. Drag a resize handle to change the size of the text area.

Editing and Selecting Type

To edit type you must go into Text Editing mode. To make changes to the character/paragraph formatting of text you must first highlight or select the text on which you want to work. You can then make changes.

Editing text

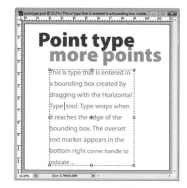

1 To edit text select the Horizontal Type tool. Click directly into the text you want to change. This takes Photoshop into Text Editing mode. Make changes using the keyboard as necessary. Click the Commit button in the Options bar to accept the changes you make and to leave Text Editing mode. Click the Cancel button in the Options bar if you do not want to keep the changes.

Selecting text

1 Make sure you are in Text Editing mode, then click and drag across the text to highlight a specific range of characters, from a single character to a word to all visible text. Double-click on a word to highlight one word. Triple-click to highlight a line of text. Click four times to select a paragraph.

2 In Text Editing mode, use Ctrl/Command+A to select all text on the layer, or choose Select>All.

3 With the appropriate range of text highlighted you can then make changes to the settings. The changes you make apply to the highlighted text only.

Character Settings

You can use options in the Options bar when the Type tool is selected, or in the Character palette to change the settings for selected text.

Font

Use the Font pop-up to choose from the list of fonts available on your system. Choose a style – such as Bold or Italic – from the Font Style pop-up.

Size

Enter a value in the Size box to change the size of your type. Points are the default unit of measurement for type in Photoshop.

Leading

Leading controls the distance from one baseline of type to the next. Enter a leading value in points in the Leading entry box. Photoshop applies a default leading value of 120% of the type size you have selected if you leave the leading set to (Auto).

My mother sang while I
was sleeping, rocked me
gentle in the cradle

Kerning and tracking

In the Character palette, you can create settings for kerning and tracking. Metrics, the default, uses the built-in pair kerning table for the font.

1 To kern character pairs, click between the characters in the text to place the text insertion bar. You can enter a value in the Kerning entry box or use the pop-up to choose a preset value. Negative values move characters closer together. Positive values move characters apart. Press Enter/Return to accept the changes made in the dialog.

Hot tip

You can choose Window>Character to show the Character/ Paragraph palette, or you can click the Palettes button ( ) in the Options bar if you have the Type tool selected.

Beware

Make sure you select a range of text before you make changes to Character settings.

143

Hot tip

If you are uncertain about which control is which in the Character palette, rest your cursor on the icon to the left of the entry box until the ToolTip label appears:

...cont'd

2 For Tracking, highlight a range of text you want to track. Enter a value in the Tracking entry box, or use the pop-up.

# AWAY
Tracking = 84

# AWAY
Tracking = -36

Baseline Shift

The Baseline Shift control allows you to move highlighted characters above or below their original baseline to create a variety of effects.

1 To baseline-shift characters, in Text Editing mode make sure you highlight the characters you want to shift.

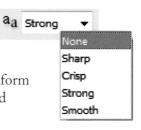

2 Enter a positive value to baseline-shift upwards, enter a negative value to baseline-shift downward.

Anti-aliasing

The anti-aliased setting in the Options bar creates type with a slightly soft edge. It does this by blurring the pixels that form the edge of the type. Use this option to avoid unnecessary jagged edges, unless you are working with very small type. Anti-aliasing text can help the type to blend into its background. Text that is not anti-aliased can look jagged. Choose an amount of anti-aliasing from the Anti-alias pop-up in the Options bar.

Type at very small sizes can appear blurred if anti-aliasing is applied.

**None
Sharp
Crisp
Strong
Smooth**

Paragraph Settings ¶

The controls in the Paragraph palette are most useful when you are working with Paragraph type consisting of one or more paragraphs. Click the Paragraph palette button, or, choose Window>Paragraph if the palette is not already showing.

1 Before you can apply Paragraph settings you must highlight the range of text on which you want to work. (See page 142.)

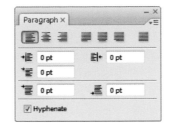

(See page 142.)

Alignment

1 To change the alignment for selected paragraphs, or a complete layer, click on one of the alignment buttons: Left, Right, Center, in the Paragraph palette or Options bar.

2 Alternatively, choose one of the Justify alignment options to justify type so that both edges of the column are straight. You cannot justify Point type. The variations for justified type affect how the last line of a paragraph is treated. Rest the cursor on the icon for a ToolTip label.

Indents

1 To set a Left, Right or First Line indent for selected paragraphs, enter a value in the appropriate entry box.

Space Before, Space After

1 To create additional space above and/or below a paragraph or range of selected paragraphs, enter a value in the Space Before and/or Space After entry boxes.

Masked Type

In essence, the Masked Type option creates a complex selection – a selection in the shape of type. This can be powerful and flexible when you want to show images through the shape of letterforms.

1 Select the Type Mask tool. Position your cursor on the image where you want the type to start. Click. This sets the text insertion point. A translucent color mask appears across the image.

2 Enter text on the keyboard. As you type the colored mask becomes transparent in the letterforms to indicate the type mask selection. Click the Commit button in the Options bar to create the selection.

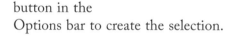
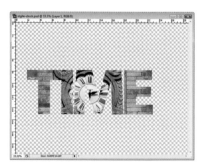

3 A type selection appears in the image window. Notice that the Type Mask tool does not create a new layer.

4 You can now drag the selection to a new image window, create a new layer from the selection or use any commands that you would typically use on a selection.

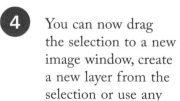

Type and Layer Styles

Layer styles can be applied to type layers whilst the type layer remains an editable type layer.

1 To apply a Layer Style to a type layer, first click on the type layer to make it active.

2 Choose Layer>Layer Styles. Select a style from the style submenu. Create settings in the Layer Style dialog box. When you OK the dialog box,

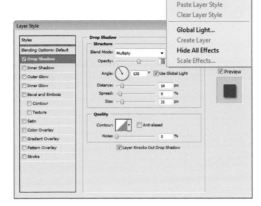

You can also select a layer style using the Add Layer Style button at the bottom of the Layers palette:

the layer in the Layers palette now has a "T" thumbnail and a *fx* icon indicating that it is an editable type layer with a layer effect applied.

See page 123 for further information on working with layer styles. See page 142 for information on working with editable type layers.

147

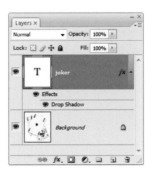

The editable type layer with layer style separated from the background layer.

Type Effects

Photoshop provides a variety of creative techniques for producing interesting effects with type.

Type on a path

You can create type that follows a path created using the Pen tool or a Shape tool.

See Chapter 10, "Paths" for information on creating paths and working with the Pen and Shape tools.

Hot tip

The baseline indicator is the squiggly line that crosses the I-beam three-quarters of the way down the cursor:

1 Select the Horizontal or Vertical Type tool. Position your cursor on the path. It is important to place the baseline indicator on the path. Click on the path. Begin typing at the text insertion point. Click the Commit/Cancel button in the Options bar to accept/discard changes. When you commit type on a path, the type appears on a new layer in the Layers palette.

2 To reposition type along the path, select the Path Selection, or Direct Selection tool. Position your cursor at the beginning of the type. When the cursor changes (⊦), click and drag to move the type along the path.

Warp Type

Photoshop provides a variety of preset type warps that you can customize to suit your requirements.

Hot tip

To flip type across a path, select the Path Selection tool, or the Direct Selection tool. Position your cursor on the type. When the cursor changes to the I-beam with arrow, click and drag the cursor across the path.

1 To warp type, make sure that you have selected a type layer in the Layers palette. Click the Warp Type button (𝕴) in the Options bar. Choose a warp preset effect from the Style pop-up menu. Use the Bend, Horizontal and Vertical Distortion sliders to control the effect. Click OK. Warped type remains editable. Choose None from the Style pop-up menu to remove warping from a type layer.

10 Paths

Paths are essential for creating cutouts for use in applications such as Adobe InDesign and can also be used to create accurate selections.

Converting Selections to Paths

A quick technique for creating a path is to make a selection, convert the selection into a work path, and then into a path.

1 First make a selection using any of the selection tools. Then, choose Make Work Path from the Paths palette menu.

2 The Make Work Path dialog box appears. Specify a Tolerance value (from 0.5–10).

3 OK the dialog box. A work path appears in the Paths palette, along with a thumbnail of the path. The selection disappears. Choose Save Path from the palette menu if you want to save this path before making any adjustments to it. Enter a name. OK the dialog box. The new path appears in the palette, replacing the work path.

4 To hide the path, click in empty space in the Paths palette. To show the path, click on the path name to select it. The path highlights.

Converting paths to selections

You can also convert a path into a selection. This is useful when you want a very accurate selection.

1 To convert a path into a selection, click on the path in the Paths palette to highlight it. Then choose Make Selection from the palette menu, or click the Load Path as Selection button.

Using the Pen Tool

You can use the Pen tool to create paths. When you start to create a path it appears as a "work path" in the Paths palette. A work path is only a temporary path.

The Pen tool creates anchor points which are connected by straight lines or curved segments. You can use the other tools in the Paths tool group to modify a path by adding, deleting or moving anchor points, and by changing the nature of the point, from smooth to corner and vice versa. You can also edit curved segments by dragging the Bézier direction points.

1 To create a path, select the Pen tool in the Toolbox. Make sure the Create Path icon is selected in the Options bar. You can select the Rubber Band option from the drop down triangle in the Options bar to see a preview of the line segments as you draw.

2 Position your cursor where you want to start drawing the path, then click, release the button, move the mouse and click again to create a straight line segment. Continue moving your cursor and clicking to create further straight line segments.

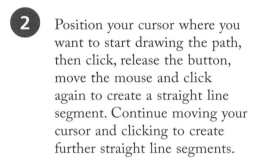

3 Alternatively, you can click and drag to set an anchor point and create direction lines for a curve segment. Then, release the button and move the cursor, and again click and drag to create the next anchor point with direction lines. Continue in this way to create the path you want. Position the Pen tool cursor at the start point. Notice the cursor now has a small circle attached to it. Click to create a closed path. The path appears in the Paths palette with the default title of Work Path.

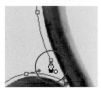

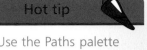
Hot tip

Use the Paths palette menu (▼≣) to create a new path before you use the Pen tool to automatically save the path without going through the intermediary stage of a work path.

Hot tip

You can press the Delete key to delete the last anchor point. Press Delete twice to delete the entire path.

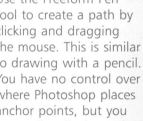
Hot tip

Use the Freeform Pen tool to create a path by clicking and dragging the mouse. This is similar to drawing with a pencil. You have no control over where Photoshop places anchor points, but you can easily edit the path after it is drawn.

...cont'd

4 To create an open path, follow the techniques outlined in steps 1–3 but instead of clicking back at the start point click on the Pen tool in the Toolbox to finish the path. This is now an open path to which you could, for example, apply a stroke.

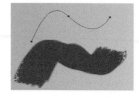

Creating corner points

As you use the Pen tool to create paths, you can draw corner points as you go, in combination with straight line segments and smooth points. In many instances, smooth points alone cannot create the shape of the path you want.

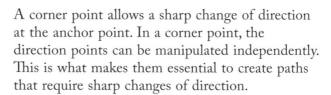

A corner point allows a sharp change of direction at the anchor point. In a corner point, the direction points can be manipulated independently. This is what makes them essential to create paths that require sharp changes of direction.

1 To draw a corner point, click and drag as you would to set a smooth point. Concentrate on getting the shape of the path coming into the point correct. Release the mouse button.

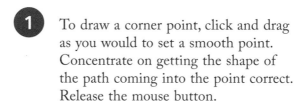

2 Position your cursor on the anchor point, hold down Alt/option, then click and drag off the point. This converts the point to a corner point. You are now controlling the direction of the outgoing curve segment. As you drag the second direction point, notice that it no longer has any effect on the incoming direction point.

3 Move your cursor to a new position, then continue drawing either smooth or corner points.

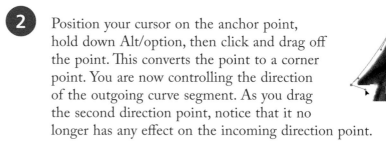

Selecting Paths and Points

Use the following techniques for selecting, deselecting and deleting paths.

1 To select a path, first you have to show it. To do this, click the path entry in the Paths palette. The path now shows in the image window.

2 To select and move an entire path, select the Path Selection tool and click anywhere on the path. All anchor points on the path highlight as solid squares. Drag an anchor point or any part of the selected path to reposition it. To deselect a path, click away from the path using the Path Selection tool. The path still shows, but is not selected.

3 To select and edit anchor points and their associated direction points, select the Direct Selection tool. Click on a visible, but not selected path to make it active. You now see the curve and line segments together with the anchor points that form the path.

4 Click on the anchor point of a curve segment to select the point The anchor point you click on becomes solid and it displays its direction points.

5 To delete a path using the Direct Selection tool, with a point or line segment of the path selected press Delete twice. Alternatively, with the entire path selected using the Path Selection tool, press Delete once. You can also drag the path name onto the Wastebasket icon in the Paths palette.

153

Don't forget

A selected anchor point is a solid square; a non-selected point is a hollow square.

Beware

To improve the clarity of these illustrations, the path has been moved away from the edge of the image.

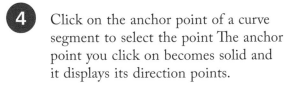

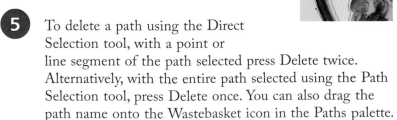

Managing Points

To achieve a precise path, you often need to add, delete and convert points on a path.

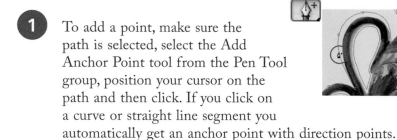

1 To add a point, make sure the path is selected, select the Add Anchor Point tool from the Pen Tool group, position your cursor on the path and then click. If you click on a curve or straight line segment you automatically get an anchor point with direction points.

2 To delete a point, make sure the path is selected, select the Delete Anchor Point tool, position your cursor on an existing anchor point then click. The path redraws without the point.

3 To convert a smooth point into a corner point, select an anchor point with the Direct Selection tool. Select the Convert Point tool, position your cursor on a direction point then click and drag. Use the Direct Selection tool to make any further changes to the direction points.

154

4 To convert anchor points on straight line segments into smooth points, select the Convert Point tool, position your cursor on the anchor point then click and drag. Direction lines appear around the point. Use the Direct Selection tool to make any further changes to the points.

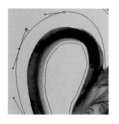

5 To convert a smooth point into a corner point without direction lines, select the Convert Point tool then click on an anchor point.

Manipulating Points

Paths invariably need to be modified and fine-tuned to produce the result you require.

1 To edit a smooth point, make sure the path is selected, then click on the anchor point to select it. Direction points appear either side of the anchor point. Direction points control the shape and length of a curve segment.

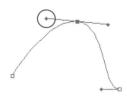

2 When you drag a direction point of a smooth anchor point, as you change the angle of one side, the other direction point moves to balance the point you are moving. This ensures the curve is always smooth through the anchor point.

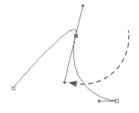

3 The further away from the anchor point you drag a direction point, the longer the associated curve segment becomes. As the curve segment is anchored at the anchor points at either end, this causes the curve segment to bow out more. Bring the direction point closer to the anchor point and the curve segment becomes shorter.

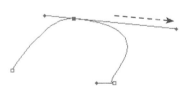

4 When you drag direction points on a corner anchor point, each moves totally independently of the other, allowing a sharp change of direction at the point.

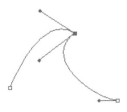

Don't forget

Select the Direct Selection tool to edit paths and points (see page 153, "Selecting Paths and Points").

Hot tip

Select an anchor point and press the arrow keys to move the selected point in 1-pixel increments.

155

Hot tip

With the Pen tool selected, hold down Ctrl/Command to toggle temporarily to the Direct Selection tool. When the cursor is positioned directly over an anchor point or direction point, hold down Alt/option to toggle to the Convert Point tool.

Exporting Paths

Exporting Clipping Paths

Create a clipping path when you want to create transparent areas in an image you intend to use in an application such as QuarkXPress or Adobe InDesign. A clipping path makes areas of the image outside the path transparent, allowing you to see past the outline of the image to the background on which the image is placed.

1 Create a saved path (see page 150). If you have more than one path in the Paths palette, make sure you select the appropriate path. Use the Paths palette menu ( ) to select Clipping Path.

New Path...
Duplicate Path...
Delete Path

Make Work Path...

Make Selection...
Fill Path...
Stroke Path...

Clipping Path...

Palette Options...

2 Use the Path pop-up to specify a different path to make into a clipping path if necessary. Enter a Flatness value.

Clipping Path
Path: vase
Flatness: | device pixels
OK
Cancel

3 When you have saved a clipping path, you need to save the file in Photoshop EPS, PDF or TIFF file format for output. Choose File>Save As. In the Save As dialog box, give the file a name and specify where you want to save it.

4 Choose Photoshop EPS or TIFF from the Format pop-up. Click Save. Clipping Paths saved with the image are automatically exported with the file when you save in Photoshop EPS or TIFF file format.

EPS Options
Preview: TIFF (8 bits/pixel)
Encoding: ASCII85
☐ Include Halftone Screen
☐ Include Transfer Function
☐ PostScript Color Management
☐ Include Vector Data
☐ Image Interpolation
OK
Cancel

5 See the section on saving in Photoshop EPS format (page 47) for information on Preview and Encoding options.

...cont'd

6 When you import the file into a QuarkXPress or Adobe InDesign page, the clipping path hides areas of the image outside the clipping path. The second version of the vase image on this InDesign page has a background and does not have a clipping path.

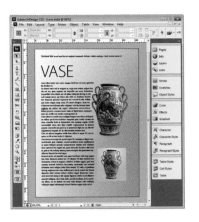

Hot tip

Save a file with a clipping path in Photoshop EPS format if you are printing the file to a PostScript output device.

Exporting paths to Adobe Illustrator

Sometimes it is useful to export a path from Photoshop into Adobe Illustrator to perform further manipulation on it.

1 To export a path to Adobe Illustrator, choose File>Export>Paths to Illustrator. In the Export Paths dialog box, change the name if necessary but leave the automatically generated .ai extension to distinguish the file. If your Photoshop document has more than one saved path, use the Paths pop-up to choose the path you want to export. Click Save.

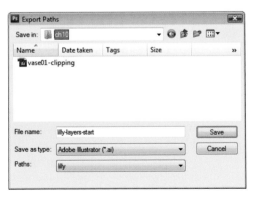

157

2 Use File>Open in Adobe Illustrator to import the path. If the path is not visible initially, use the Selection tool to select within the crop marks then apply a fill or stroke to the path.

Hot tip

When you open exported paths in Adobe Illustrator, the crop marks indicate the dimensions of the original Photoshop image.

3 See pages 36–37 for information on placing an Illustrator EPS into Photoshop.

Creating Shape Layers

The Shape tools allow you to create lines, rectangles and ovals, as well as polygons and custom shapes. Use the Options bar to set specific options for each tool individually.

1 To draw a rectangle as a Shape layer, first choose a foreground color for the shape. Select the Rectangle tool. Make sure the Shape Layer button is selected in the Options bar.

2 Position your cursor in the image window. Drag diagonally to define the size of the shape. A new Shape layer appears in the Layers palette. To create additional shapes on the same Shape layer, either choose a new shape tool from the Options bar or use the same tool. Select the Add to Shape Area button in the Options bar. Draw the shape.

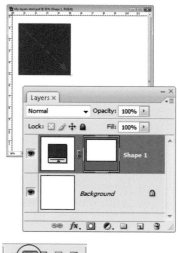

3 To draw a square, hold down Shift then drag with the Rectangle tool. Release the mouse button before you release Shift, otherwise the constraint effect will be lost. Hold down Alt/option then drag with the Rectangle tool to draw a rectangle from the center out.

4 Select the Shape layer icon (a highlight border appears around the Shape layer icon), then use the Direct Selection tool to select and then make changes to the shape of the object in the image window.

11 Channels and Masks

Channels and masks bring powerful and creative capabilities for manipulating images with precision and control.

Quick Mask Mode

In Quick Mask mode you create a 50% red, semi-transparent overlay. This overlay represents the protected area of the image. The overlay is similar in concept to a traditional rubylith mask. Quick Mask mode is particularly useful because you can see both the image and the mask as you create and fine-tune the mask.

1 To create a quick mask, click the Edit in Quick Mask Mode button in the Toolbox. Make sure that the default foreground and background colors are black and white respectively.

2 Show the Brushes palette and choose a brush size. Use a hard-edged brush to create selections with a clearly defined edge. Use a soft-edged brush to create selections that are slightly softer along the edge. Select a painting tool and drag across your image to "paint" in the mask. Painting with black adds to the mask. Although you see through the 50% red mask, the pixels covered by the mask are completely protected.

3 To remove areas from the mask you can use the Eraser tool, or paint with white.

4 When you are satisfied with your mask, click the Edit in Standard Mode button. This turns the areas of the image that were not part of your quick mask into a selection. You can now make changes to the selected areas (in this example on the left the Lens Blur filter has been applied), leaving the areas that were the quick mask unchanged.

The Channels Palette

The Channels palette (Window>Channels) shows a breakdown of the color components that combine to make up the composite color image that you work with most of the time on-screen.

For example, in RGB mode, there are four channels – the composite image (all the other channels combined), and then a channel each for the red, green and blue color components of the image. In CMYK mode, there are five channels.

Using the Channels palette you can be selective about which of the color components in your image you change.

1 To switch to a specific channel, click the channel name in the Channels palette. The channel highlights to indicate that it is selected. The image window changes according to the channel you chose.

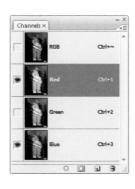

2 You can view additional channels by clicking the Eye icon for a channel. The image window changes, but your editing remains limited to the selected channel.

3 Click on the composite RGB channel to return to normal image-editing view.

Hot tip

You can change the display of channels from grayscale to the color they represent by choosing Edit>Preferences> Interface (Windows), or, Photoshop> Preferences>Interface (Mac). Select the Show Channels in Color checkbox:

161

Beware

Indexed Color mode, Grayscale mode and Bitmap mode all have only one channel.

Save and Load Selections

Beware

An alpha channel is an 8-bit grayscale channel, which means that every time you save a selection as a channel, you are adding to the file size of your image.

Because you can only have one "active" selection in an image at any one time, the facility to store a selection which can be reloaded later is vital, especially if the selection is complex and took some time to create. You save selections as an extra channel in the Channels palette. These extra channels are referred to as "alpha channels".

Saving selections

1 To save a selection to a channel, make your selection on the image, then choose Select>Save Selection. The Save Selection dialog box appears. Specify in which document you wish to save the channel. (You can save channels in another document to keep the file size of the current document as small as possible.) Leave the Channel pop-up on New. Enter a name for the channel. Click OK. Alternatively, make your selection and then click the Save Selection button in the Channels palette.

2 An additional channel appears in the Channels palette. This is the new "alpha channel". An alpha channel is a grayscale channel.

3 When you have saved a selection to an alpha channel you can freely deselect the selection in your image, as you can now reselect exactly the same area at any time using the alpha channel.

Loading selections

Use the following process to reselect an area using the alpha channel:

1 To load a channel as a selection on the image, make sure the composite image is displayed. You can do this by clicking on the topmost channel name in the Channels palette. Then choose Select>Load Selection. The Load Selection dialog box appears.

2 Use the Channel pop-up menu to specify which channel you want to load. Select an operation as appropriate.

The operations allow you to control how the selection you are about to load interacts with any existing selection in the image – adding to it, subtracting from it or intersecting with it. Click OK.

3 Alternatively, using the Channels palette, drag the channel you want to load onto the Load Selection icon.

4 To delete a channel, drag the channel name onto the Wastebasket icon at the bottom of the palette.

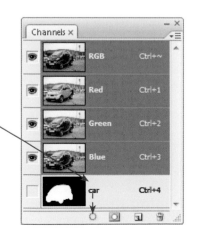

Hot tip

File formats that can retain alpha channel information when you save include: Photoshop, PDF, PICT and TIFF.

Hot tip

When you are working in Quick Mask mode, you can turn the quick mask into an alpha channel by dragging the quick mask entry that appears in the Channels palette onto the New Channel icon:

Editing Alpha Channel Masks

You can display an alpha channel without loading it onto the image as a selection. You can then edit the mask by painting with black, white or gray.

1 In the Channels palette. Click on the alpha channel you want to display. The channel name highlights and an eye icon in the left column of the palette, indicates that this is the visible channel.

2 The image window changes from the composite view to a grayscale representation of the mask. The white area represents the selection and the black portions represent the protected areas.

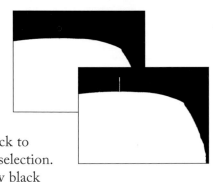

3 To edit an alpha channel, select a painting tool and brush size. Click the Default Colors icon if necessary, to change the foreground color to black. Paint with black to remove areas from the selection. Paint with white on any black portion of the mask to add it to the selection.

Reshaping masks

Another useful technique for editing a selection mask is to view a mask and image simultaneously by turning the alpha channel selection into a colored mask (very much like using Quick Mask

...cont'd

mode) and then reshaping the mask by painting with black, white or shades of gray.

1 To reshape a mask, ensure you don't have an active selection on your image. Click on the alpha channel in the Channels palette to select it. It highlights and

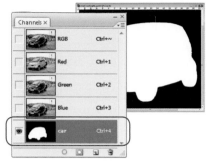

the Eye icon shows on the left. The image window now displays the grayscale selection channel mask. The Eye icon disappears from the Composite RGB channel and from the individual Red, Green and Blue channels.

2 Click in the currently empty Eye icon position for the Composite channel. The eye appears for the Composite channel and in the individual Red, Green and Blue ones. The Composite channel now also shows in the image window but only the alpha channel is selected – indicated by the highlight.

3 The image window changes in appearance. The selection area appears as normal whilst the protected or masked portions of the image have a quick mask type transparent film applied.

4 Select the Brush or Pencil tool. Paint with white to remove areas of the image from the mask (to enlarge the unmasked area). Paint with black to add portions of the image to the mask.

Hot tip

Typically, when you edit masks, you paint with black or white, with the Mode set to Normal and an Opacity of 100%. However, you can reduce the opacity or pressure settings in order to create a partial mask.

Beware

Make sure that the Eye icon for an alpha channel mask is not selected, then click the Composite channel when you want to return to the standard editing view.

Layer Masks

For information on creating layers, see Chapter 8. For information on using filters, see Chapter 13.

Use layer masks to hide or reveal areas of a layer. A layer mask is extremely useful because you can use it to try out effects without actually changing the pixels on the layer. When you have achieved the result you want, you can apply the mask as a permanent change. If you are not satisfied, you can discard the mask without having permanently affected the pixels on the layer.

This example begins with an image with two layers. The original Background layer and a layer created using the Render>Fibres filter.

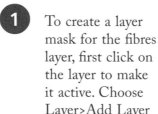
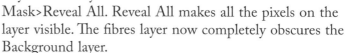

1   To create a layer mask for the fibres layer, first click on the layer to make it active. Choose Layer>Add Layer Mask>Reveal All. Reveal All makes all the pixels on the layer visible. The fibres layer now completely obscures the Background layer.

2   In the Layers palette, the layer mask is active, indicated by the highlight border on the mask thumbnail. Click on the layer thumbnail to make the layer active. Click on the Layer Mask thumbnail to continue editing the mask.

You can have only one layer mask per layer.

3   With the layer mask thumbnail selected, make sure that the foreground color is set to black. Choose a painting tool and start painting. Painting with black hides pixels on the fibres layer, revealing pixels on the Background layer.

4 Pixels on the fibres layer are not permanently erased when you paint with black. Paint with white to show pixels on the fibres layer – in effect hiding pixels on the Background layer. (If you choose Layer>Add Layer Mask>Hide All, you start with the opposite scenario to the above. Now all the pixels on the fibres layer are hidden. Paint with white to reveal pixels on the fibres layer, paint with black to hide them.)

5 To temporarily switch off the layer mask, choose Layer>Layer Mask>Disable, or hold down Shift then click on the Layer Mask thumbnail. To reactivate the mask, choose Layer>Layer Mask>Enable, or hold down Shift then click again on the Layer Mask thumbnail.

6 To apply the layer mask as a permanent change, choose Layer>Layer Mask>Apply.

Reveal All
Hide All
Reveal Selection
Hide Selection

Delete
Apply

Disable
Unlink

7 To discard the layer mask, without affecting pixels on the layer, choose Layer>Layer Mask>Delete. Or, drag the Layer Mask thumbnail (not the Layer thumbnail) onto

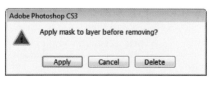

the Wastebasket icon in the bottom of the palette. Click Apply or Delete. Once you apply a layer mask you lose the flexibility of making further changes – the effect is fixed. Click Delete only if you want to discard the mask.

Channel and Quick Mask Options

The Channel Options dialog box and the Quick Mask Options dialog box allow you to control the color of a mask and whether the protected or unprotected area of the image is colored with the overlay.

1 To change channel options, double-click the alpha channel thumbnail. Alternatively, with the alpha channel selected, use the Channels palette menu (▾☰) to choose Channel Options.

2 In the Channel Options dialog box you can enter a new name for the channel. You can also choose Selected Areas to reverse the way in which the color will apply. In other words, masked (protected) areas will appear white, while the selection area (unprotected) will appear black.

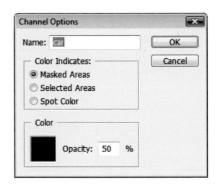

3 To change the color used to represent the masked (protected) area and its opacity, click the Color box and choose a new color from the Color Picker.

4 To change the settings for a quick mask, double-click the Quick Mask Mode icon in the Toolbox, then make the appropriate changes in the dialog box that appears.

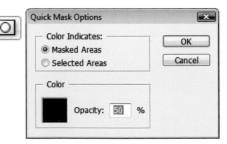

12 Color Adjustments

Color correction involves making changes to the overall brightness and contrast, and also the color balance, in an image, to compensate for any tonal deficiencies and color casts in the original.

Brightness/Contrast

The Brightness/Contrast command provides the least complicated controls for changing overall brightness/contrast levels in an image. It does not change individual color channels; it makes the same adjustment to all pixels across the full tonal range of the image.

1 To change brightness and contrast for an entire image, or for a selection, choose Image> Adjustments> Brightness/ Contrast. Drag the Brightness and Contrast sliders or enter values in the entry boxes. OK the dialog box.

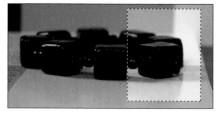

2 Choose Image>Adjustments>Auto Contrast to automatically adjust the contrast for an image or selection. Highlights should appear lighter and shadows darker, giving an overall improvement to the image. Auto Contrast does not adjust individual channels. It makes highlights appear lighter and shadows darker by mapping the lightest and darkest pixels in the image to white and black respectively.

Auto Levels and Auto Color

Auto Levels allows you to adjust brightness and contrast automatically. Auto Levels examines each color channel independently and changes the darkest pixels to black and the lightest pixels to white, then redistributes the remaining shades of gray between these two points.

Auto Levels works best on images that have a reasonably even distribution of tonal values throughout the image, as it redistributes pixels based on white and black points, with a tendency to increase contrast.

Auto Color removes unwanted color casts in an image without adjusting the contrast in an image.

1. To apply Auto Levels to an image, choose Image>Adjustments>Auto Levels. (Use Edit>Undo if the result is not satisfactory.)

2. To apply Auto Color to an image, choose Image>Adjustments>Auto Color. (Use Edit>Undo if the result is not satisfactory.)

Hot tip

You can also use the Auto Levels command from within the Levels and Curves dialog boxes. Click the Auto button.

Beware

Auto Levels adjusts each color channel in the image individually. As a result, it may remove or sometimes introduce color casts.

171

Original   Auto Levels   Auto Color

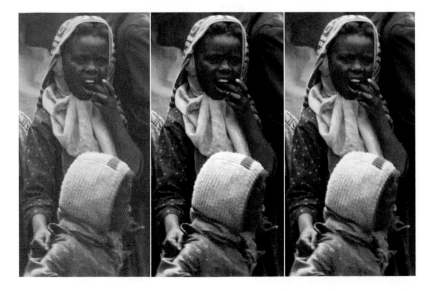

Don't forget

Both Auto Levels and Auto Color generally produce good results, but they do not allow the precision of the manual adjustments that you can make using the Levels and Curves dialog boxes.

The Levels Dialog Box

Use the Levels dialog box (Image>Adjustments>Levels) to adjust the tonal balance for color and grayscale images. You can adjust highlight, shadow and midtone ranges for a selection or an entire image, or you can make changes to individual channels only.

Input Levels

The Input Levels sliders and entry boxes allow you to improve the contrast in a "flat" image.

Don't forget

The most flexible way of working with Levels, Curves and Color Balance is to set up Adjustment layers (see page 120). Adjustment layers allow you to repeatedly adjust settings in the respective dialog boxes until you are satisfied with the result.

1 Use the Channel pop-up menu to select a channel. If you do not select an individual channel, you can work on the composite image and affect all channels.

2 To darken an image, drag the solid black slider to the right. Alternatively, enter an appropriate value in the leftmost Input Levels entry box. This maps pixels to black. For example, if you drag the black slider to 15, all pixels with an original value between 0 and 15 become black. The result is a darker image.

Hot tip

The spiky graph in the middle of the Levels dialog box is a Histogram. See pages 176–177 for an explanation of the Histogram in the Levels dialog box.

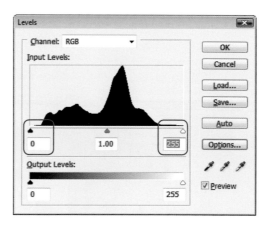

Don't forget

Dragging either or both the black or white Input Levels sliders inwards has the effect of increasing contrast in the image.

3 To lighten an image, drag the hollow, white Input Levels slider to the left. Alternatively, enter an appropriate value in the rightmost Input Levels entry box. The result is to map pixels to white. For example, if you drag the white slider to 245, all pixels with an original value between 245 and 255 become white. The result is a lighter image.

Gamma

The gray triangle and the middle Input Levels entry box control the Gamma value in the image. The Gamma value is the brightness level of mid-gray pixels in the image.

1 To lighten midtones, drag the gray slider to the left, or increase the Gamma value in the Input Levels entry box above the default setting of 1.00.

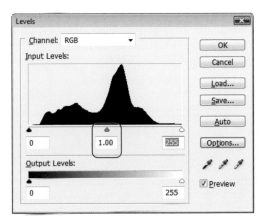

Hot tip

When you OK the Levels dialog box, you can use Edit>Undo/Redo a number of times to evaluate the changes.

2 To darken midtones, drag the gray slider to the right, or decrease the Gamma value in the Input Levels entry box.

Hot tip

See page 171 for an explanation of Auto Levels and the Auto button.

Output Levels

You can use the Output Levels entry boxes or sliders to decrease the amount of contrast in an image. Typically, you do this to target highlight and shadow values to match the output capabilities of a particular printing press, with the aim of preserving highlight and shadow detail.

1 Drag the black Output Levels slider to the right to lighten the image and reduce the contrast.

2 Drag the white Output Levels slider to the left to darken the image and reduce the contrast.

Hot tip

For RGB and CMYK images, use the Channels pop-up menu to make tonal adjustments to individual channels. Work with a calibrated monitor to ensure consistent and predictable results.

The Curves Dialog Box

The Curves dialog box (Image>Adjustments>Curves) offers the most versatile set of controls for making tonal adjustments in an image. The central brightness graph in the dialog box displays the original and adjusted brightness values for pixels in the image. The graph is a straight line from 0 (black) to 255 (white) before any adjustments are made – input and output values for pixels are the same.

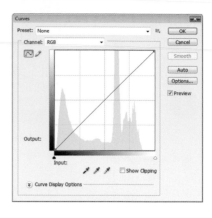

The horizontal axis of the graph represents the original or input values, the vertical axis represents the output or adjusted values. By adjusting the brightness curve, you are remapping the brightness values of pixels in the image.

Beware

For RGB images the default brightness bar along the bottom edge of the graph starts black and graduates to white. In this state, the brightness curve indicates the brightness values of colors in the image; the brightness curve starts at 0, for black, and moves to 255, for white.

Click the Curve Display Options button (⊗) then select the Pigment/Ink % radio button to reverse the display.

1 To add a point to the curve, select the Point tool. Click on the curve. (You can add up to fourteen points.) Drag the point(s) around to edit the curve. Or, click at a point in the graph and the curve will change according to where you clicked.

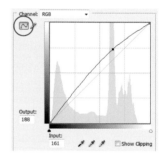

2 To delete a point, click on a point to select it, then press the Delete/Backspace key. You can also drag it outside the Brightness graph.

3 To lighten or darken an image, select the Point tool, position your cursor near the midpoint of the graph, then click to place a new point. Click and drag this point upwards to lighten, downwards to darken.

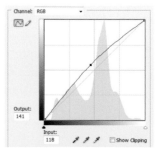

Hot tip

Click the Curve Display Options button (⊗) then use the Simple/Detailed Grid buttons to display gridlines in 25% or 10% increments respectively:

4 To increase the contrast in an image, place a point at roughly the ¼ tone part of the graph and drag this upwards to lighten the highlights. Next, place a point at roughly the ¾ tone part of the graph. Drag this downward to darken the shadow areas. The result is to increase the contrast in the image by lightening the highlights and darkening the shadows, whilst leaving the midtones more or less untouched.

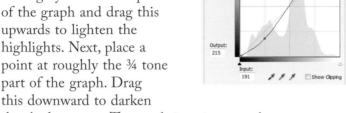

5 Reverse the setting in step 4 to decrease the contrast in an image.

6 To limit changes to the midtones and highlights, click on the graph to place a point at the ¾ tone. Place a point at the ¼ tone and drag this upwards. Reverse this procedure to change midtones and shadows without affecting highlights.

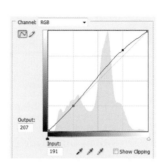

7 Move the black point/white point sliders inwards to increase overall contrast in an image as you can do in the Levels dialog box. (See pages 172–173 for further information.) Deselect Histogram in the Curve Display options to hide the histogram.

8 Click the Curve Display Options expand button to reveal further options for controlling the appearance of the dialog box as you change settings.

> **Curve Display Options**
>
> Show Amount of: ● Light (0-255)
> ○ Pigment/Ink %
>
> Show: ☑ Channel Overlays ☑ Baseline
> ☑ Histogram ☑ Intersection Line

Hot tip

Hold down Alt/option, then click on the Reset button (previously Cancel) to restore the original settings in the dialog box.

Hot tip

Select a point on the graph, then press the arrow keys on your keyboard to move the point in increments.

Hot tip

Use the Channels pop-up to edit the baseline curve for individual color channels. It is important to work with a calibrated monitor to accurately assess the impact of changes you make to individual color channels.

With Channel Overlays selected in Curve Display Options, changes to individual color channels are visible in the composite brightness graph.

The Histogram Palette

A histogram is a bar chart that represents the distribution of pixels in an image. Shadows are on the left side of the histogram, highlights on the right and midtones in the middle. The spread of pixels through the shadows, midtones and highlights represents the tonal balance in an image.

Having the Histogram palette visible as you work on an image can help you evaluate the effect of the changes and adjustments you make.

1 The Histogram palette is grouped initially with the Navigator and Info palettes. Click the Histogram tab, or choose Window>Histogram to show the palette.

2 Choose Expand View from the Histogram palette menu ( ) to enable access to the Channel drop down menu. Choose from RGB, Luminosity, and Colors to view the histogram for the channel you specify. For an image with more than one layer you can choose Selected Layer from the Source drop down menu to view a histogram for the pixel content on the currently active layer.

3 Choose All Channels View to display an extended palette with histograms for all channels in the image, with the exception of Alpha channels, Spot channels and masks. The topmost histogram represents the luminance, or overall brightness values for the composite channel.

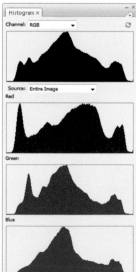

4 For RGB and CMYK images you can choose Colors from the Channel drop down menu to display a composite histogram of the individual color channels in color.

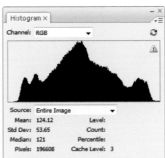

Beware

When in All Channels view, choosing an option from the Channels drop down menu changes the top histogram only.

5 To show statistical information for the histogram, choose Show Statistics from the Histogram palette menu. Move your cursor through the bars of the histogram itself to get readouts for Level, Count and Percentile in the statistics area.

6 When working in dialog boxes such as Levels and Curves, provided that the Preview option is selected, the Histogram palette updates as you make changes to the settings in the dialog box.

7 The Cached Data warning icon appears when the Histogram palette display is based on information held in cache (an area of short term memory) rather than the actual current state of the image. To ensure that the histogram represents all pixels in the image in their current state, either click the Cached Data warning icon, or click the Uncached Refresh button. You can also double-click anywhere within the histogram. Photoshop uses cached information for the image in order to display information in the histogram quickly, but slightly less accurately, as the cached information is based on a representative sampling of pixels in the image only.

Shadow/Highlight Command

The Shadow/Highlight command is useful for images with strong backlighting resulting in a silhouette effect on the foreground elements. The default settings in the Shadow/Highlight dialog box are intended to improve images with backlighting problems. You can also use the Shadow/Highlight command to lighten shadows.

1 To adjust shadows and highlights in an image, choose Image>Adjustments>Shadow/Highlight.

2 Drag the Shadows Amount slider to the right, or enter a value in the percentage entry field from 0–100 to lighten the shadows. The

higher the value the greater the degree of lightening.

3 Drag the Highlights Amount slider to the right to darken the highlights. You can also enter a value in the percentage entry field. The higher the value the greater the degree of darkening.

Before

After

Match Color Command

Use the Match Color command when you need to make colors in one image (the destination image), consistent with colors in another image (the source image). You can also use this command to match colors between layers within the same image.

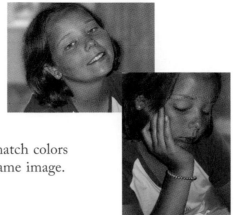

Hot tip

The Match Colors command can be useful when you need to match skin tones in one image to the overall color tones in another image.

1 To match colors in an image to colors in a different image, select the destination image. Choose Image> Adjustments> Match Color. If the destination image has multiple layers, make sure you select the layer you want to match before you choose the Match Colors command.

Hot tip

Make sure you have the Preview option selected in order to see how changes you make in the Match Color dialog box affect the destination image.

2 In the Image Statistics area of the dialog box, use the Source drop down menu to select the source image which contains the color characteristics you want to match. If necessary, use the Layer drop down menu to select a specific layer within the source image, or leave the option set to Merged to use the overall color statistics of the source image.

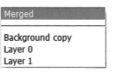

...cont'd

3 In the Image Options area of the dialog box, drag the Fade slider to reduce the intensity of the color adjustment in the target image if necessary. Drag the Luminance slider to increase or decrease the brightness of the result. Drag the Color Intensity slider to increase or decrease the overall color saturation.

Matching colors between layers

1 To match color characteristics from one layer to another in the same image, make sure you have the destination layer (the layer whose color you want to change) selected.

2 Choose Image>Adjustments>Match Color. In the Image Statistics area set the Source drop down menu to the name of the file with which you are working.

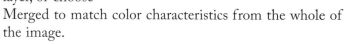

3 From the Layer drop down menu select a specific layer, or choose Merged to match color characteristics from the whole of the image.

4 Use the Fade, Luminance and Color Intensity sliders to fine tune the results.

Black & White Command

For converting an image to black and white, the Black & White command offers much greater flexibility and control than using Image>Mode>Grayscale. By adjusting values for specific color components in the image you can enhance or tone down areas of an image as required.

Hot tip

You can use the Black & White command as an adjustment layer. (See pages 120–121 for further information.)

1 To convert an image to black and white, choose Image>Adjustments> Black & White.

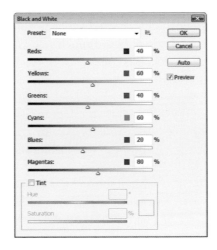

2 Either select a preset conversion from the Preset pop-up menu, or use the color sliders to adjust the proportions of each color to be used in the conversion. Drag sliders to the right to darken, to the left to lighten, the gray tones in the image.

3 If required, you can select the Tint checkbox to apply a color tone to the image. Drag the Hue slider to change the color of the tint. Use the Saturation slider to increase/ decrease the amount or strength of the tint color.

Hot tip

Click the Auto button to create a conversion which maximizes the distribution of gray values in the original image. You can then continue to adjust the sliders to achieve the final result you want.

181

Original	Image>Mode >Grayscale	Black & White (High Contrast Red preset)	Tint

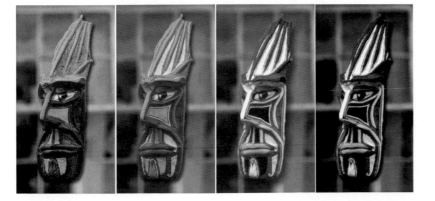

Hot tip

Position your cursor inside the image itself, then drag to target and adjust specific color ranges within the image.

Color Balance

Like the Brightness/Contrast command, the Color Balance dialog box provides general controls for correcting an overall color cast in an image. As such, it provides the least complex method of color correction.

The Color Balance dialog box works on the principle of complementary colors. If there is too much cyan in an image, you drag the Cyan–Red slider towards red to remove the cyan color cast. If there is too much magenta, drag the Magenta–Green slider towards green.

Don't forget

Work on the composite view of an image when using the Color Balance dialog box.

1 To adjust the Color Balance of an image, choose Image> Adjustments> Color Balance. Click the Shadows, Midtones or Highlights radio button to specify the tonal range to which you want to make changes.

2 Drag the color sliders to reduce/ increase the amount of a color in the image.

Beware

You should use the Color Balance dialog box with caution, and only if your monitor is calibrated accurately, as you need to be certain that the color adjustments you see on screen accurately represent colors at final output.

Preserve Luminosity

Select this option to prevent brightness values from changing as you change color levels. This helps maintain the overall color balance in the image.

13 Filters

Filters add enormous creative flexibility and potential to image-manipulation, and it is well worth spending some time experimenting with them. You can use filters across an entire image, or you can apply them to selections or layers to limit the results to specific areas. Photoshop ships with more than 100 filters as standard.

Filter Controls

Use the Filter menu to access the Photoshop filters. Many of the filters have standard controls, which are explained below. Some filters, such as Filter>Stylize>Solarize, do not display a dialog box, but apply the effect immediately. Other filters take you into the Filter Gallery dialog box where you create and preview settings.

1 Click the Preview check box to see the effect of your settings previewed in the main image window, as well as in the Preview window inside the filter dialog box.

2 Click and drag on the image in the Preview window to scroll around to preview different parts of the image. Alternatively, with the filter's dialog box active, position your cursor in the main image window – the cursor becomes a hollow box – then click to set the view in the Preview window.

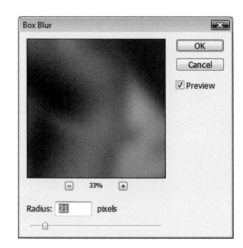

3 Click the "+" or "-" buttons to zoom in or out on areas of the image. You can also use the Ctrl+Spacebar (Windows) or Command+Spacebar (Mac) keyboard shortcuts within the Preview window or the image window.

4 Hold down Alt/option and click the Reset button (previously Cancel) to revert to the original settings in the dialog box.

5 After you OK a filter's dialog box, use Ctrl+F (Windows) or Command+F (Mac) to reapply the last-used filter and its settings.

Unsharp Mask and Sharpen Filters

These filters allow you to enhance detail in your images.

Unsharp Mask

This is a powerful function which can help you to sharpen blurry images in specific areas. For example, if you rotate an image, or change the dimensions or resolution of the image, it may blur due to any interpolation that Photoshop applies. Where the Unsharp Mask filter finds edges (areas where there is a high degree of contrast), it increases the contrast between adjacent pixels. The result is to create an apparent improvement in the focus of the image.

1 To use Unsharp Mask to sharpen an image, choose Filter> Sharpen>Unsharp Mask. The Unsharp Mask dialog box appears.

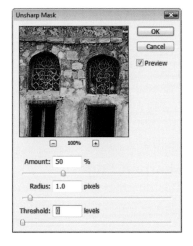

2 Adjust settings for Amount, Radius and Threshold. Evaluate changes you make to settings in the Preview window within the dialog box and in the image window itself. Click OK or press Return/Enter.

Set the zoom percentage of the document window to 100% to get an accurate preview of the effect of sharpening in the image. Also, it is preferable to evaluate final results in the actual document window, rather than in the Unsharp Mask preview window.

Amount – Use this to control the amount of sharpening applied to the edges (minimum = 1, maximum = 500). The picture will become pixelated if the amount is too high.

Values below 50% produce subtle results; values between 50% and 200% produce moderate results; while values between 200% and 500% produce dramatic, exaggerated results.

The settings for Radius and Threshold need to be taken into account when setting the Amount value (see the next page).

...cont'd

Radius – Radius controls the depth of pixels along the high-contrast edges that are changed.

A low radius value restricts the impact of the filter; higher values distribute the impact. Radius values of 2.0 or lower usually produce acceptable sharpening.

Threshold – Sets a level for the minimum amount of contrast between pixels an area must have before it will be modified. The Threshold value is the difference between two adjacent pixels – as measured in brightness levels – that must occur for Photoshop to recognize them as an edge.

High Threshold values limit changes to areas where there is a high degree of color difference. Use low values to apply the filter more generally throughout the image.

Sharpen and Sharpen More

Use the Sharpen and Sharpen More filters when an image becomes blurred after resampling. Both filters work by increasing contrast between adjacent pixels throughout the image or selection. Sharpen More has a more pronounced effect than Sharpen.

Sharpen Edges

This filter has a more specific effect, applying sharpening along high-contrast edges. In effect, it has a less global impact on a selection or image than Sharpen and Sharpen More.

Hot tip

On high-resolution images, use a Threshold value of around 8 or higher to limit the sharpening effect to specific areas.

Sharpen   Sharpen Edges   Sharpen More   Unsharp Mask

Smart Sharpen

The Smart Sharpen filter uses advanced algorithms to produce enhanced sharpening results using an easy to use dialog box with an expanded Preview window, which makes it easier to evaluate the effect of settings on the image.

1 Choose Filter>Sharpen>Smart Sharpen.

2 Set values for Amount and Radius. Amount controls the degree of sharpening. Higher values increase the amount of contrast between neighboring pixels, producing the visual effect of increased sharpness in the image. Radius controls how far the results of sharpening extend into surrounding pixels.

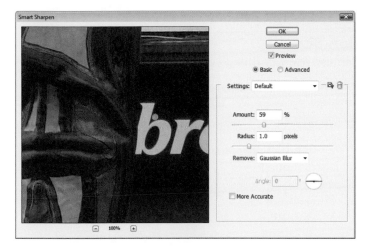

3 Choose an option from the Remove pop-up menu. Each option uses a different algorithm to sharpen the image. Gaussian Blur uses the same method as the Unsharp Mask filter. Lens Blur attempts to detect detail where it then increases sharpening, typically producing fewer halos. Use Motion Blur to lessen blur caused by movement of the subject. When you select Motion Blur, set the angle control to specify the direction of the blur.

4 Select the More Accurate checkbox to get the best results, although this can take slightly longer to process.

Don't forget

Sharpening works by increasing contrast where there is already edge detail. Using too much Sharpening in an image can cause halos and other unwanted artifacts to appear in the image.

187

Hot tip

To achieve greater control over sharpening in shadow and highlight areas of an image, select the Advanced radio button. Use the Fade slider in the Highlights and/or Shadows tabs to reduce the overall impact of the sharpening settings specifically in the shadow and highlight tonal ranges.

Blur Filters

The Blur filters reduce the contrast between adjacent pixels along edges where considerable color shifts occur, to create a softening, defocusing effect. Blurring produces the opposite effect to sharpening – which increases the contrast between adjacent pixels.

"Blur" and "Blur More" blur a selection in preset amounts offering only a limited degree of control. For greater control when blurring you can use the Gaussian Blur option, which blurs according to a bell-shaped Gaussian distribution curve.

To Blur a Layer or Selection

1 Create a selection if you want to limit the effect of the Blur filter to a specific area of your image. Choose Filter>Blur>Blur, or Filter>Blur>Blur More.

Motion Blur

You can use Motion Blur to create the effect of a moving subject or camera.

Angle = 0,
Distance = 12

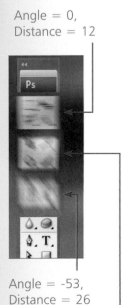

Angle = -53,
Distance = 26

Angle = -45,
Distance = 12

1 To create a motion blur, make a selection, if required. Choose Filter>Blur> Motion Blur.

2 Enter a value in the Angle box, or drag the Angle indicator to specify the angle or direction of the blur. Enter a value in the Distance entry box to specify the distance in pixels for the blur effect. OK the dialog box.

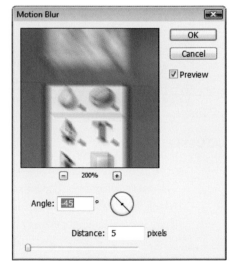

188

Radial Blur

Radial Blur creates the effect of zooming in as you take a picture.

1 To create a radial blur, make a selection if required. Choose Filter>Blur>Radial Blur.

2 Select a Blur Method and Quality, and specify an Amount (0–100). Click and drag in the Blur Center window to specify the center point for the zoom or spin effect. OK the dialog box.

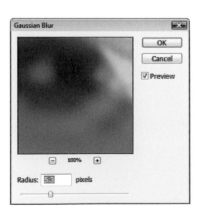

Amount – This value determines the distance pixels are moved to create the blur effect. Higher values produce more intense effects.

Zoom – Zoom creates a zoom-like blurring effect.

Spin – Spin rotates and blurs pixels around a central point.

Quality – Good and Best produce better, smoother results due to the interpolation methods used, but take longer.

Gaussian Blur

1 Use Gaussian Blur to control the degree of blurring. Gaussian Blur adds low frequency detail to the image or selection. Choose Filter>Blur>Gaussian. Use the Radius slider to adjust the amount of blurring.

Beware

If you are working on a layer, make sure the Transparency lock is deselected if you want the blur to take effect along the edges of the layer's pixels. (See page 119.)

189

Hot tip

The Box Blur filter blurs an image or selection using an average color value for neighboring pixels. Increased radius settings create greater blurring. This filter can produce interesting creative effects.

Noise Filters

Add Noise filter
The Add Noise filter randomly distributes high-contrast pixels in an image, creating a grainy effect.

1 To add noise, create a selection, select a layer or work on the entire image. Choose Filter>Noise>Add Noise. Specify Amount, Distribution and Monochromatic options.

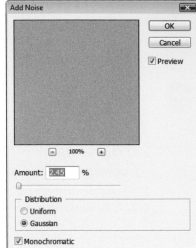

Hot tip

Add Noise is a good way to begin creating textured backgrounds.

Amount – Determines the degree to which pixels are changed from their original color. Enter a number from 1–400.

Uniform – Produces an even spread of pixels.

Gaussian – Produces a more dramatic result.

Monochromatic – Choose Monochromatic to distribute grayscale dots.

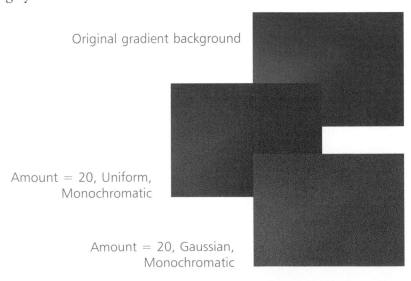

Original gradient background

Amount = 20, Uniform, Monochromatic

Amount = 20, Gaussian, Monochromatic

Dust & Scratches filter

Use the Dust & Scratches filter to remove small imperfections and blemishes in a scan caused by dust and scratches. The degree of success you have with this filter depends largely on the image or selection you apply it to.

1 To remove dust and scratches, create a selection or work on the entire image. Choose Filters>Noise>Dust & Scratches. Specify Radius and Threshold settings. Click OK.

Radius – Determines how small a blemish must be for it to be worked upon by the filter. For example, at a radius of 3 pixels, the Dust & Scratches filter will not attempt to make changes to imperfections above this size.

Threshold – Specifies the minimum amount of contrast between pixels there must be before changes are made.

Despeckle filter

This produces the opposite effect to the Add Noise filter, smoothing and blurring the image, but having little effect on edges.

Median filter

The Median filter also removes noise from a poor-quality scan. It works by averaging the color of adjacent pixels in an image.

1 To use the Median filter, create a selection, or work on the entire image. Choose Filter>Noise>Median. Specify a Radius value (1–100). OK the dialog box.

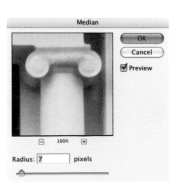

Reduce Noise Filter

Image noise is often apparent in images captured on budget digital cameras and in images saved using high JPEG compression settings. The Reduce Noise filter attempts to remove unwanted noise artifacts whilst retaining edge detail.

1 To remove noise artifacts, choose Filter>Noise>Reduce Noise. Drag the strength slider to increase or decrease the overall impact of the filter on the image. This affects all channels in the image.

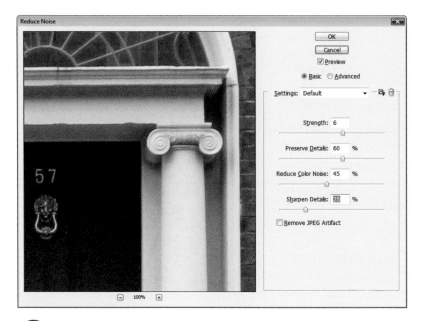

2 Create the settings you require to reduce the appearance of noise artifacts. Either drag the sliders to control the settings, or enter a value in the % entry boxes. High Preserve Details settings retain detail along edges and in areas such as hair, but lead to less noise reduction overall in the image. Reduce Color Noise removes random color pixels.

3 Select the Remove JPEG Artifact checkbox to compensate for noise typically found in images saved using high JPEG compression settings.

192

The Extract Command

Use the Extract command to isolate an object from its background; especially useful when the object has edges that are not clearly or distinctly defined, such as hair. Make sure you are working on a layer to use the Extract command. If you perform the Extract command on the Background layer it becomes Layer 0 when you OK the dialog box.

1 To extract an object from its background, choose Image>Extract.

2 Select the Edge Highlighter tool. In the Tool Options area, set a brush size and choose a color for the edge highlight from the Highlight pop-up.

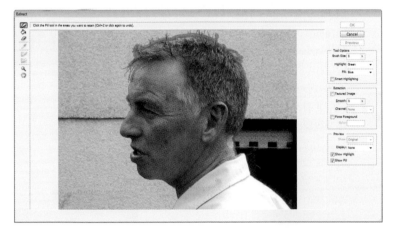

3 Zoom in on the image if necessary, then draw around the object you want to extract to define the edge. It is important to create a highlight that slightly overlaps both the edge of the foreground object and its background. Use a larger brush size to completely cover more delicate, intricate, "wispy" areas of the foreground object, such as hair; use a smaller brush size to highlight sharper, more defined edges.

...cont'd

194

Hot tip

Use the Zoom and Hand tools as you would in the Photoshop image window. (See page 24 for further information.)

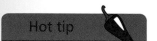

Hot tip

When you have filled an interior area with the Fill tool, clicking again in the fill area clears the fill.

Hot tip

Use the Smooth control in the Extraction area, if necessary, to improve the result of the extraction. The Smooth control can help remove stray artifacts from the extraction by feathering edges slightly.

4 Use the Eraser tool to undo any mistakes you make with the Edge Highlighter tool. You can use the Undo command within the Extract dialog box to undo the last brush stroke.

5 Make sure you completely enclose the object if it has a well-defined interior. It is not necessary to highlight edges where the object touches the edge of the image window.

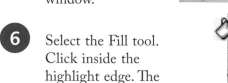

6 Select the Fill tool. Click inside the highlight edge. The interior fills with the Fill color set in the Tool Options area of the dialog.

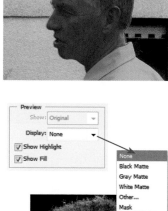

7 Click the Preview button to preview the results. Use the Display pop-up in the Preview area to set the background against which you see the extracted object. It can help to preview against more than one background color to pick up on any problem areas, before you click OK. (See page 195 for techniques to refine the extraction area.)

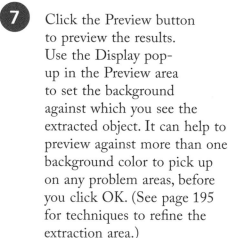

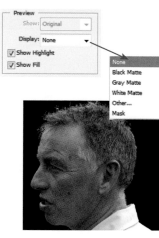

8 Use the Show pop-up to switch between the original and extracted images. Again, this is useful for making decisions about the results of the extraction before you OK the dialog box.

9 OK the dialog box to complete the extraction.

Fine Tuning Extractions

After you preview the results of the extraction, you will need to fine-tune it, before you OK the dialog box.

1 To make adjustments to the extraction, select the Show Highlight option in the Preview area. The original highlight edge reappears. Choose Original from the View pop-up. The solid background against which you preview the results of the extraction disappears and the original background pixels reappear.

2 Use the Eraser tool to erase parts of the highlight edge and use the Edge Highlighter tool to redefine areas of the edge, as necessary.

3 When you finish editing the highlight edge, select the Fill tool, then click inside the edge to recreate the fill area. Click the Preview button to preview your changes. Repeat the editing process as necessary until you are satisfied with the result.

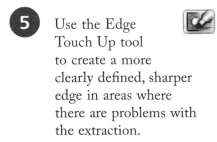

4 If there are still problems with the extraction, switch off the edge highlight. Use the Clean Up tool to remove any unwanted pixels around the extraction after you preview it. Hold down Alt/ option, then drag with the Clean Up tool to refill any unwanted gaps in the extracted object.

5 Use the Edge Touch Up tool to create a more clearly defined, sharper edge in areas where there are problems with the extraction.

6 Click OK to finish the extraction.

The Liquify Dialog Box

Don't forget

Use the Zoom and Hand tools as you would in the standard Photoshop image window.

The Liquify dialog box allows you to create a wide variety of distortions for retouching images or for achieving creative effects. The dialog box has tools that can push, pull, rotate, reflect, pucker and bloat areas of the image.

1 To distort an entire layer, select the layer, or make a selection on a layer to define an area for distortion. Choose Filter>Liquify.

2 Freeze areas of the image that you don't want to change using the Freeze Mask tool. Set a Brush size, then drag across areas of the image you want to freeze. Frozen areas appear as a semi-transparent, red mask. Use the Thaw Mask tool to make frozen areas editable again.

Beware

You must rasterize a Type layer or a Shape layer before you can use the Liquify command.

3 Select a tool with which to distort the image, then set tool options. (See the facing page for information on the tools.) Choose a brush size from the Brush Size slider. Set a brush pressure. Lower pressure settings distort the image more slowly allowing you more control over the distortion. Brush Density controls the softness of the edge of the brush. Choose Turbulent Jitter settings to control how tightly the Turbulence tool distorts pixels.

Don't forget

Only the active layer is distorted by the Liquify dialog box.

4 Drag in the image to create the distortion. You can press the left mouse button without dragging the mouse to create effects with tools such as the Twirl tools. Set a Brush Rate to control the speed at which distortions happen when you keep the mouse still. Click OK to accept the changes.

Liquify Distortion Tools

There are 7 distortion tools to choose from. Remember to create tool settings for Brush size, Pressure and Turbulent Jitter before you use the tools. Distortions are most pronounced at the center of the brush area. You can create distortions by dragging across pixels, or simply by holding down the left mouse button.

Hot tip

Use the Reconstruct tool to restore pixels to their original state:

1   Use the Forward Warp tool to distort pixels in a forward direction as you drag.

2   Use the Turbulence tool to smoothly mix or scramble pixels. This can sometimes create interesting cloud and wavelike effects.

3   Use the Twirl Clockwise tool to rotate pixels around the brush area in a clockwise direction. Hold down Alt/option to twirl in a counter clockwise direction.

4   Use the Pucker tool to concentrate pixel detail into the center of the brush area.

5   Use the Bloat tool to disperse image detail away from the center of the brush.

6   Use the Mirror tool to copy pixels into the brush area. The tool reflects the area perpendicular to the direction of the stroke.

7   Use the Push Left tool to move pixels to the left when you drag upward, to the right when you drag downward.

Hot tip

Hold down Alt/option then click the Restore all button to revert to the original state of the image.

Pattern Maker

Use the Pattern Maker plug-in to generate patterns based on a selected area of an image. You can create and preview multiple pattern variations until you find one you like.

1 Open an image that will provide the sample pixels for the pattern. Choose Filter>Pattern Maker.

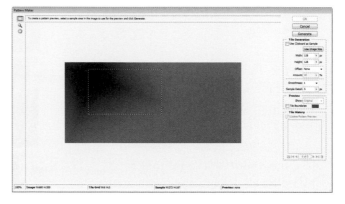

2 Use the Selection tool to create a selection to form the basis of the pattern. Click the Generate button to preview the results.

3 Experiment with settings in the Tile Generation area of the dialog box. Then click the Generate Again button. Repeat the process as required.

4 Use the Tile History controls to move backward and forward through the patterns you have generated. OK the dialog box when you have created a pattern you want to utilize.

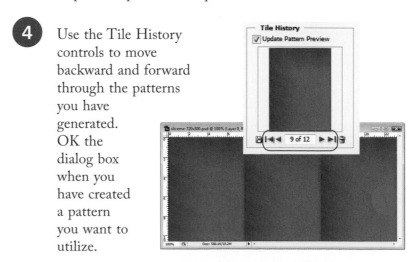

Filter Gallery

The Filter Gallery allows you to preview and apply individual or multiple filter effects to an entire image, a layer or a selection.

1 To show the Filter Gallery, choose Filter>Filter Gallery. A preview of the image, with the currently selected filter applied, appears on the left of the window.

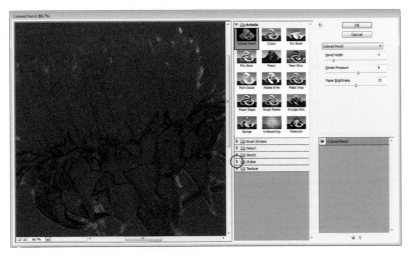

2 Click the Reveal/Hide triangle for each filter category to show or hide the filters available for that category.

3 Click a filter thumbnail to apply it to the preview. Use the individual controls on the right hand side of the window to experiment and create the settings you want to use. Each filter effect has its own, specific set of controls.

4 In the Preview area, use the "-" or "+" buttons, or the zoom pop-up to zoom in or out on an area of the preview. Position your cursor in the preview area, then click and drag to reposition the preview.

Beware

The Filter Gallery is not available for images in CMYK color mode.

Beware

Not all Photoshop filters are available from within the Filter Gallery.

Hot tip

Choosing many of the individual filters from the various sub-menus in the Filter menu brings you into the Filter Gallery. For example, choose Filter>Artistic then select any of the filters to access the filter's controls in the Filter Gallery.

...cont'd

5 Use the Reveal/Hide button (⊗) to hide the filter thumbnails area to create a larger preview area if necessary. You can choose filters by name from the Filter drop down menu if you hide the thumbnails.

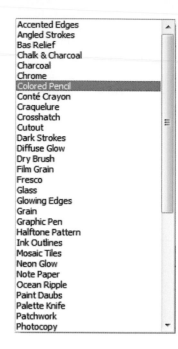

6 To apply more than one filter to the preview, click the New Effect button (▣) at the bottom of the window, then click on another filter effect thumbnail. The new filter is added to the bottom of the filter effect list.

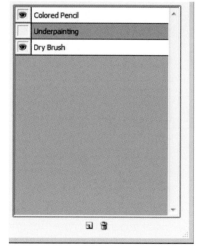

7 In the Filter effect list area, click the Eye icon box to apply or hide the filter effect. Drag the filter effect upward or downward to change the order in which the filters are applied. Drag a filter effect into the Wastebasket to remove it.

8 OK the Filter Gallery dialog box when you are ready to apply the settings.

Vanishing Point

The Vanishing Point filter makes it possible to maintain accurate and correct perspective when you edit an image that contains perspective planes. Use the filter to define a perspective grid, or plane, to establish a vanishing point. You can then make edits within the grid that conform to the correct perspective.

1 To edit in perspective, choose Filter>Vanishing Point. To define a perspective grid, select the Create Plane tool.

2 Position your cursor on the image, then click to set the first node for the plane. Move you cursor to a new position (do not hold down the mouse button and drag). Click to set the next node. Repeat the process to set a third and fourth corner node. The grid appears in blue in the Vanishing Point window.

3 A blue bounding box indicates a valid grid. If the grid or bounding box turns yellow or red as you create or edit it, there is a problem with the alignment of the perspective plane. Typically, the plane doesn't line up correctly with perspective in the image. To correct this, select the Edit Plane tool (), position your cursor on a corner node of the perspective grid, then to adjust the grid to line up with elements in the image.

Hot tip

To delete a perspective grid, select the Edit Plane tool, then press the Backspace or Delete button.

Hot tip

Working with the Create Plane tool, use the Grid Size pop-up to specify the frequency of the grid:

Choose Show Edges from the palette menu ( ) to control the visibility of the perspective grid.

Hot tip

Using the Create Plane tool, hold down Ctrl/ Command then drag a center top/bottom, or center left/right node to define an additional perpendicular plane.

...cont'd

4 To change the size of the perspective grid rectangle, make sure you drag either the center left/right, or center top/bottom handle.

Removing objects in perspective

1 Create a perspective grid then select the Stamp tool. The grid disappears, to facilitate editing, but the bounding box remains visible. Create settings for the diameter, hardness and opacity of the brush in the Options bar. (See Chapter 5, "The Painting Tools", for information on these controls).

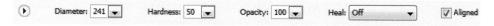

2 Position your cursor over the source pixels – the area you want to use as a sample point. Hold down Alt/option, then click the mouse button to set the sample point, then release the Alt/option key.

3 Reposition you cursor over the target pixels – the area in the image where you want to paint out detail with pixels from around the sample point. Notice as you move your cursor towards the rear of the perspective grid that the cursor size changes to match the grid and maintain the correct perspective.

4 Click and drag to remove unwanted detail. Repeat steps 2–4, if necessary, in order to use slightly different sample points so that the result appears in keeping with the rest of the image and as natural as possible.

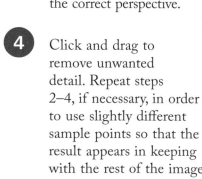

Editing Perspective Planes

Using the Vanishing Point filter you can create additional perspective planes that conform to the same perspective as the original plane. Initially planes "tear off" at 90° angles. You can paste content into Vanishing Point and manipulate it so that it conforms to the perspective grid.

1 Begin by creating the initial, or parent, perspective plane. Select the Edit Plane tool. Hold down Ctrl/Command, then drag a center left/right, or center top/bottom node to create a new, child plane at 90°.

2 If you need to change the angle of the new plane to match the content of the image, enter an angle in the Angle entry box, or drag the Angle slider. To adjust the angle manually, hold down Alt/option, then drag the center node opposite the axis of rotation.

3 To paste content into perspective planes defined in Vanishing Point, make sure you copy the content to the clipboard before you choose Filter>Vanishing Point. When you paste content into Vanishing Point it appears as a "floating" selection. Drag the selection into a plane and it transforms into perspective. Click outside the selection to deselect it and apply the perspective transformation.

When you have overlapping planes in Vanishing Point, use Ctrl/Command+click to select through planes in the stacking order.

Beware

You cannot change the angle of a "parent" perspective plane after you create a "child" plane from it.

Smart Filters

Smart Filters work with Smart Object layers. Using Smart Filters you can work with filters non-destructively on an image – making changes to the filter settings as often as required.

Beware

You cannot apply Extract, Liquify, Pattern Maker and Vanishing Point filters as Smart Filters.

1 If you are working with an image consisting only of a background layer, duplicate the layer first. Otherwise, select the layer to which you want apply a smart filter.

2 Choose Filter>Convert for Smart Filters. This converts the layer into a smart object layer to which you can then apply smart filters.

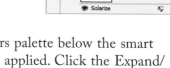

3 Apply a filter from the Filter menu. The smart filter icon appears on the smart object layer to indicate the presence of smart filters. The smart filter layer mask icon and the smart filter appear in the layers palette below the smart object layer to which they are applied. Click the Expand/Collapse triangle to show/hide smart filters for the layer.

Hot tip

You can apply more than one filter as a smart filter.

4 Double-click the smart filter name to edit the filter settings. Click the eye button to hide/show the smart filter settings on the image.

5 Using the smart filter layer mask you can apply the smart filters selectively on the smart object layer. Make sure you click the layer mask icon to select it before you attempt to edit the layer mask. For example, you could load a selection, then fill it with black to remove the smart filter effect in the area defined by the selection. (See pages 166–167 for information on working with layer masks.)

Hot tip

You can control opacity and blending mode for the smart filter by double-clicking the Edit Blending Options button (🔀) for the smart filter layer.

14 Web and Multimedia

This chapter looks at some of the considerations for using different image types effectively in formats suited to the environment of the World Wide Web. It also covers techniques for using images in multimedia work.

Save for Web & Devices

The Save for Web & Devices command offers comprehensive controls for saving images to be used on the Web. Use the Save for Web & Devices command when you want to create an image file size that is as small as possible – to ensure the fastest possible download times – without sacrificing too much quality.

1 Choose File>Save to save any changes you have made to the image in the current file format. Then choose File>Save for Web & Devices.

2 In the Save for Web & Devices dialog box, click the 2-Up tab to compare the original image and the image with optimization settings applied. Click the Optimized tab to view the image with optimization settings applied. When viewing 2-Up and 4-Up, each optimized pane indicates file format, size, and approximate download time for a specific modem speed in the annotations area.

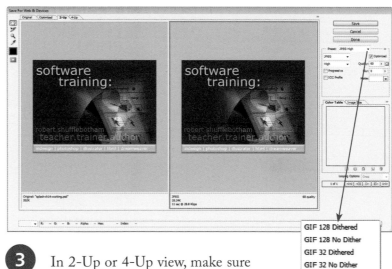

3 In 2-Up or 4-Up view, make sure the Optimized pane is selected – indicated by a blue border. In the Optimize panel, choose an optimization level from the Presets pop-up menu. The Optimized image pane updates so that you can evaluate different options.

...cont'd

4 In 4-Up view, choose Repopulate Views from the Presets palette menu to update the remaining panes with lower quality optimization settings.

Optimization: 4-Up View

The 4-Up tab is particularly useful because it allows you to preview images using a variety of optimization levels before you decide which level of optimization you want.

1 Click the 4-Up tab to view the Original image, the image optimized using the current optimization settings set in the Optimization panel, and two lower quality variations of the current optimization settings.

2 To use one of the lower quality comparison panes as the Optimized image, click inside the pane to select it. A blue highlight border on the pane indicates that it is selected. Choose Repopulate Views from the Optimization panel pop-up menu. The selected pane becomes the Optimized image. Its optimization settings appear in the Optimization area. The comparison panes update with lower quality optimization settings.

3 To compare different, unrelated optimization settings, click on a comparison pane to select it, then choose an optimization setting from the Settings pop-up. In this case, make sure you do not use the Repopulate Views command.

Saving Optimized Images

You can preview an optimized image in a Web browser before you make a final decision on which optimization settings to use. This can be a useful check before committing yourself to saving the file.

1 Choose a browser from the Browser Preview pop-up from the bottom of the dialog box. The browser

launches
and displays
the image
from the
selected
pane. Image
details
such as
file format,
dimensions
and file
size are
listed below
the image.
Below
the image
details is the

HTML code necessary to display the image.

2 To save an optimized image, select the pane with the settings you want to use. Click Save in the Save for Web & Devices dialog box.

3 Use standard Windows/ Macintosh techniques to navigate to the folder in

File name:	splash-ch14-working
Save as type:	Images Only (*.jpg)
Settings:	Default Settings
Slices:	All Slices

which you want to save the image. Enter a file name for the image. The file extension for the optimization settings is automatically appended to the file name. The file is saved using the current settings in the Optimize panel.

4 Select HTML and Images from the Save as Type pop-up menu, to generate the code necessary to display the image in a separate HTML file. This file is automatically

named and saved in the same folder as the optimized image. The optimized image is saved in an images folder which Photoshop creates automatically within the folder you specify.

5 To specify whether the HTML file uses a table, or Cascading Style Sheets to display an image with slices, choose Other from the Settings pop-up menu. Choose Slices from the pop-up menu. Create the settings you require in the

Slice Output area of the Output Settings dialog box.

6 For images that contain slices, use the Slices pop-up menu to choose whether to save all slices in the image, or only the currently selected slice. Each slice is saved as a separate file and named according to the settings in the Output Settings dialog box.

7 To change the way in which slices are named, in the Output Settings dialog box choose Saving Files from the pop-up menu. Use the File Naming pop-ups to make changes.

GIF Optimization Settings

The GIF file format usually provides the most efficient and flexible optimization controls for images which have areas of flat color, with sharp edges and type, as you often find in logos and buttons.

1 To optimize an image using GIF file format, select the image pane for which you want to create the settings. To create a setting for a slice, use the Slice Select tool to select a slice.

2 Choose one of the preset GIF settings from the Preset pop-up menu. Or, to create custom GIF settings, choose GIF from the Format pop-up, then specify settings using the options in the palette.

3 Drag the pop-up Lossy slider or enter a value to reduce file size by discarding color information. Values of 5–10 can often be applied without noticeably degrading the image quality. Choose a color palette (see pages 214–215) and a dither method (see page 216).

4 Use the Colors pop-up menu to specify the maximum number of colors in the Color palette. Increase the Web Snap setting to shift colors to their closest Web palette equivalents to help avoid dithering in a browser.

5 Select Transparency to preserve any transparent areas in the image. You can choose a Matte color if you want to blend the edges of transparent areas into the background of a Web page. Use the Transparency pop-up to choose a dither type for the blended areas if required.

JPEG Optimization Settings

JPEG optimization works best on continuous-tone images such as photographs. JPEG compression can preserve more detail in photographic-type images than GIF and still provide considerable file size reduction.

1 To optimize an image using JPEG file format, select the image pane for which you want to create the settings. To create a setting for a slice, use the Slice Select tool to select a slice.

2 Choose one of the preset JPEG settings from the Preset pop-up menu. Or, to create custom JPEG settings, choose JPEG from the format pop-up, then specify settings using options in the palette.

3 Use the Quality pop-up to choose a quality setting, or drag the pop-up Quality slider. Use a high setting to preserve most detail in the image with a larger file size. Reduce the quality setting to achieve greater compression and a smaller file size but with reduced image quality.

4 Select the Optimized checkbox to create JPEGs with a slightly smaller file size. Some older browsers do not recognize this setting. Choose Progressive to cause the image to download to the browser in a number of passes, each pass building more detail into the image until it downloads completely. Use Blur settings, if required, to allow greater compression on the file. Settings of less than 0.5 are recommended.

5 JPEG compression does not support transparency in images. You can fill transparent areas with a Matte color to simulate transparency, provided you know the background color against which the image will be viewed.

JPEG compression is "lossy". In order to make the file size of an image smaller, some image data is discarded, reducing the quality of the image.

211

Hot tip

For medium to high JPEG compression settings, you can use a small Blur value, e.g. 0.1 to 0.5 to blur pattern artifacts that may appear along sharp edges. Higher values may reduce image detail noticeably.

PNG File Format

PNG is a relatively new file format for saving images for use on the Web. There are 2 PNG file format options: PNG-8 and PNG-24.

PNG-8

PNG-8 file format uses 8-bit color which allows a maximum of 256 colors in an image. It is most effective at compressing areas of solid, flat color, typically found in line art, logos and illustrations with type.

PNG-8 is a lossless compression formula – no color information is lost during compression. Depending on the image, PNG-8 compression can produce files 10–30% smaller than the same image compressed using GIF format.

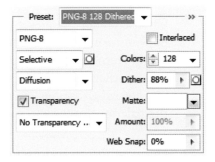

PNG-8 file format can support background transparency and background matting. Background matting enables you to blend the edges of an image into the background color you set as the background color of your Web page.

PNG-24

PNG-24 supports 24-bit color which allows millions of colors in the image. Like JPEG, this is a good format when you want to preserve subtle transitions in tone and color in a photographic type image.

PNG-24 uses a lossless compression formula – no color information is discarded during compression. As a result, PNG-24 file sizes are typically larger than if you save the image using JPEG file format.

PNG-24 supports background transparency and background matting. PNG-24 also supports multilevel transparency which allows greater control over the way in which an image blends into the background color of a Web page.

Indexed Color Mode

Indexed Color mode is an important factor in the preparation of images for use on the World Wide Web and in multimedia applications. It provides an efficient method for reducing the size of a color image. When you work on RGB color images in Photoshop, these are typically 24-bit images, capable of displaying over 16 million colors. Indexed Color Mode converts images to single channel, 8-bit images, capable of displaying a maximum of 256 colors.

Don't forget

You can convert RGB or Grayscale images to Indexed Color mode.

1 To convert an RGB color image to Indexed Color mode, choose Image>Mode>Indexed Color.

2 Use the Palette pop-up to specify a color palette which controls and limits the colors that will be used in the image. (See the next page.)

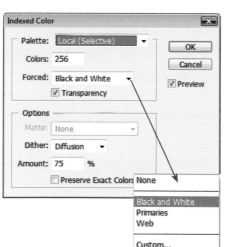

Hot tip

Make a selection before you convert to Indexed Color mode, to weight the color table towards the colors that occur in the selection.

213

3 Choose an option from the Forced pop-up to force the inclusion of certain colors in the color table.

4 Select Transparency to preserve any transparent areas in the image. Deselect Transparency to fill transparent areas with the Matte color. White is used if there is no Matte color selected. Matte is only available if there are areas of transparency. (See page 217 for more information.)

Hot tip

For Uniform, Perceptual, Selective and Adaptive color palettes you can set an exact number of colors to include. Enter a value below 256.

5 Set dithering options. (See page 216).

Color Palettes

A color palette controls the 256 possible colors that exist in an Indexed Color, GIF or PNG-8 image. Photoshop uses three methods for creating color tables in images: dynamic, fixed and custom.

Dynamic – Perceptual, Selective and Adaptive color palettes are created dynamically. Each time you optimize the image, the palette created is based on the colors occurring in the image. Different images will generate different palettes.

Fixed – the Web, Mac OS, Windows, Black & White and Grayscale color palettes are fixed. There is a limited, or fixed range of colors. If your optimization settings specify fewer than 256 colors, this reduced range of colors is drawn from the fixed color table.

Custom – Custom palettes use colors created or modified by the user. Existing GIF and PNG-8 files also have custom palettes.

System palettes
This is the standard, 8-bit system palette of either the Macintosh or Windows system.

Exact
If the image you are converting already has fewer than 256 colors, Exact is the default. The actual number of colors is indicated in the Colors entry box. You cannot dither an Exact palette.

Restrictive (Web)
This is a palette reduced to 216 or fewer colors. Use this palette to achieve consistency across different platforms and when you want to use more than one image on the same Web page. Images which are based on different color palettes can look artificial when seen side by side.

Uniform

This palette is based on a uniform sampling of colors from the color spectrum.

Adaptive

This palette is built around the colors that actually occur in an image. For individual images, it gives better results than Web, as the color table is created by sampling colors from the most frequently occurring areas of the color spectrum in the image.

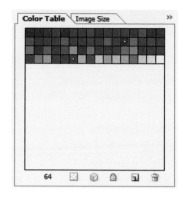

Custom

This option allows you to create your own custom color table. You can add colors (), lock colors (🔒) as well as map colors to their nearest web-safe color (📦) or transparency (🔲) using the buttons at the bottom of the Color Table palette.

Perceptual

The Perceptual option creates a color palette biased towards colors to which the human eye is most sensitive.

Selective

This is similar to Perceptual, but biased towards broad areas of color in the image and also the preservation of Web colors. Selective is the default.

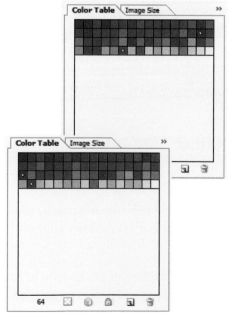

Hot tip

Indexed Color Mode converts images to single channel, 8-bit image, capable of displaying a maximum of 256 colors. To convert an RGB color image to Indexed Color mode, choose Image> Mode>Indexed Color.

Dithering

Dithering is a technique used to simulate colors that are not actually in the color palette. On computer monitors that support only 256 colors, dithering takes place to simulate a greater range of colors in an image than the monitor is actually capable of displaying. For Web images this is referred to as browser dither.

Dithering juxtaposes pixels of different colors to create the illusion of additional colors.

You can choose a dithering method for an image when you optimize it. This is referred to as application dither – the dither is built into the image.

 Hot tip

You can minimize the occurrence of browser dither, by creating the image using only Web-safe colors.

1 For GIF images, in the Save for Web & Devices dialog box, choose an option from the Dither pop-up. For Diffusion, set a Dither Amount. Higher values result in more dithering which creates the appearance of a greater number of colors in the image. Higher values can also increase the file size, depending on the image.

No Dither
No dithering is applied to the image.

Pattern
This creates a square dither pattern, similar to halftones, to simulate colors not available in the color table.

Diffusion
The results of Diffusion are usually less noticeable than Pattern as the dithering is spread across a range of pixels.

Noise
Applies a random dither pattern. This option can be used for images with slices.

Hot tip

Images with areas of solid color may compress best with Dither set to None. Images with gradients usually need dithering to prevent obvious banding.

Save As JPEG

JPEG is a compression format, widely used for preparing images for the World Wide Web. Use JPEG when you are working with photographic-type images, and when preserving color detail and quality in the image are more important than download time considerations. JPEG does not allow transparency, and file sizes may be larger than for images exported in GIF format, depending on the compression level you choose.

1 To save an image in JPEG format, choose File>Save As. Specify a location, enter a name, then choose JPEG from the Formats pop-up. OK the dialog box.

2 Choose a color from the Matte pop-up to simulate background transparency in the image. You need to know the background color of the Web page, in order to match the matte color to it.

3 Use the Quality pop-up to specify the amount of compression, or drag the slider. "Maximum" gives best quality, retaining

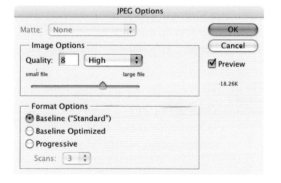

most of the detail in the image, but least compression. "Low" gives lowest image quality, but maximum compression.

4 For Format Options, choose Baseline Optimized to optimize the color quality of the image. Select Progressive and enter a number for Scans to download the image in a series of passes which add detail progressively until the image is completely displayed. Click OK to export the file.

217

Web Photo Gallery

The Web Photo Gallery command allows you to set up a website that features your images, quickly and simply, without the need to write any HTML. The website has a home page with thumbnail image links to other pages with full-size images, and includes navigation buttons.

1 To create a Web Photo Gallery choose File>Automate>Web Photo Gallery.

2 Choose a template to control the look and feel of the website from the Styles pop-up menu. A thumbnail of the style appears on the right of the dialog box. Include an e-mail address if you want viewers to be able to contact you via e-mail.

3 In the Options area, use the pop-up menu to specify settings for text labels on the site, and to specify size and compression settings for thumbnail and full-size images.

4 Click the Browse button to navigate to the folder which contains the images you want to include on the website. Click the Destination button to navigate to the folder in which you want Photoshop to create the website. Click OK, then test the Web Photo Gallery in a browser.

Device Central

Use Adobe Device Central to preview and test content you create for mobile devices. You can access Adobe Device Central from Photoshop's New and Save for Web & Devices dialog boxes, or as a standalone application.

Whenever possible it is best to create artwork intended for a mobile device at the correct size from the outset. You can achieve this from Photoshop's New dialog box.

Hot tip

Choose Devices>Check for Device Updates to download the latest profile information available for devices.

1 Choose File>New. In the New dialog box, click the Device Central button.

2 In Device Central's Available Devices panel, select a make and model. Click the expander (⊞) to reveal a list of models for a particular manufacturer. Click a specific model. The New Document tab displays default Color Mode, bit-depth, resolution and document size information for the selected device. Click the Create button to create a new Photoshop document using these settings.

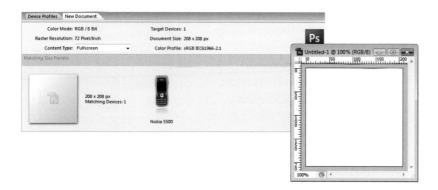

Previewing and Testing in Device Central

The Save for Web & Devices dialog box allows you to preview the artwork you create in Photoshop in a simulation environment.

1 Create artwork in Photoshop as close to the required final size as possible. Choose File>Save for Web & Devices. Create optimization settings for the image. (See pages 208–209 for information on optimizing images.)

...cont'd

2 Click the Device Central button. In the Available Devices panel, select a make and model. Click the expander (⊞) to reveal a list of models for a particular manufacturer. Double-click a specific model to display it in the Emulator panel.

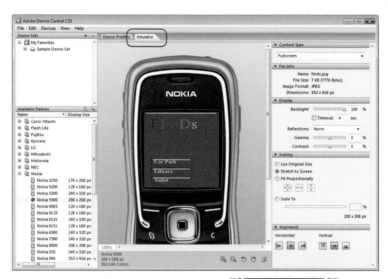

Hot tip

Click the Device Profiles tab along the top of the dialog box to access technical specifications for the selected device, including its support for Flash, Bitmap, Video and Web formats.

3 Use Display panel controls to simulate lighting scenarios such as reflections and varying amounts of backlighting. Gamma affects the overall lightness/darkness and you can also make changes to the contrast.

4 Choose one of the standard scaling options to fit the image to the display size, or use the Scale to slider to set a custom scale amount.

5 Select Alignment controls to test image alignment options.

15 Animations and Slices

Animations are built from a series of GIF images which can be played in succession to create movement and change in a Web image.

Slicing allows you to sub-divide an image into specific "slices" – which can be reformed on a Web page.

Creating a Simple Animation

Animations can range from the very simple to the very complex. Try to keep your animations simple at the outset. Remember that animation effects, if used indiscriminately on Web pages, can be distracting and as a result lose their intended impact.

Hot tip

To avoid confusion as you create an animation, make sure that you have created and finished editing all the objects and layers you want to use, before you start to build the animation.

1 Create an image in Photoshop. Use layers as the basis for the animation. The layers you create form the basic building blocks for the animation. Put elements you want to animate on separate layers.

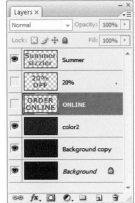

2 Hide any layers containing elements you do not want to appear at the start of the animation.

Hot tip

Choose Window> Workspace>Web Design to create a convenient arrangement of palettes for building animations and other web effects.

3 Choose Window> Animation to show the Animation palette. Photoshop adds an extra row of animation options to the Layers palette when you show the Animation palette. The current state of the image appears as frame 1 in the palette.

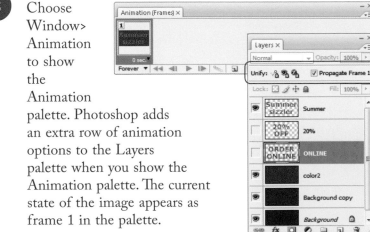

4 Choose New Frame from the palette's pop-up menu, or click the New Frame button. This creates frame 2, which is a duplicate of the preceding frame.

New Frame
Delete Frame
Delete Animation

Copy Frame
Paste Frame...

Select All Frames

Go To ▶

Tween...
Reverse Frames

Optimize Animation...

Make Frames From Layers
Flatten Frames Into Layers
Match Layer Across Frames...

Create New Layer for Each New Frame
New Layers Visible in All Frames

Palette Options...

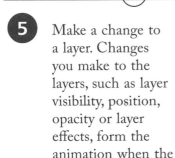

5 Make a change to a layer. Changes you make to the layers, such as layer visibility, position, opacity or layer effects, form the animation when the frames are viewed in quick succession. In this example one text layer is hidden and a different one revealed.

223

6 Repeat Steps 3-4 as necessary.

Beware

Any changes you make on a layer that affect actual pixel values – for example, painting, changing color or tone, or using transform commands – will affect all frames in the animation in which the layer is present.

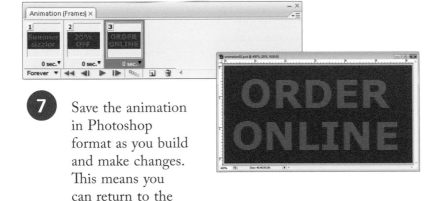

7 Save the animation in Photoshop format as you build and make changes. This means you can return to the original file, if necessary, to make further adjustments. (See page 226 for information on saving an optimized version of the animation for use on the Web.)

Playing and Managing Frames

As you build an animation you will need to preview it and to control aspects such as looping and frame rate.

1 To play an animation, click the Play button. The animation plays in the image window and each frame in the Animation palette highlights in sequence as the animation plays. Click the Stop button to stop the animation at the current frame.

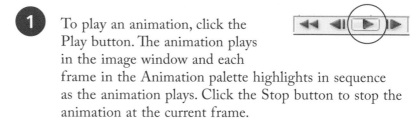

2 To select a frame, click on the frame in the Animation palette. The frame highlights and becomes the current frame. The current frame is displayed in the image window. It is the frame that can currently be edited.

3 To delete a frame, first click on it to select it. Then click the Wastebasket button at the bottom of the palette. Alternatively, drag the frame into the Wastebasket, or choose Delete Frame from the palette menu.

New Frame
Delete Frame
Delete Animation

4 To change the position of a frame, select the frame you want to move, then drag it to a new location. Release the mouse when you see a thick black bar at the position to which you want to move the frame.

5 To set the frame delay rate (the speed at which frames advance), first select a frame or multiple frames. Use the Frame Delay pop-up located below each frame. Either choose a value from the preset list, or choose Other then specify a delay in the Set Frame Delay dialog box.

6 To specify looping options, use the Loop pop-up in the bottom left corner of the Animation palette. Forever plays the animation in a continuous loop. Choose Other to specify a set number of times you want the animation to play. Enter a value in the Play ... times field.

Copying and pasting frames

You can copy a frame or multiple frames and then paste the copied frame(s) into a new location in the current animation, or into a completely different animation.

1 To copy a frame, first select the frame. A white highlight indicates the frame is selected. Choose Copy Frame from the Animation palette menu.

2 Select a frame at the location where you want to paste the copied frame. Choose Paste Frame from the Animation palette menu. Choose an option for Paste Method then click OK.

Hot tip

For a selected range of frames you can choose Reverse Frames from the palette menu to run the frames backwards. This would be useful after pasting the frames in the example on the left.

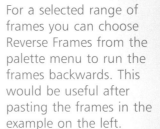

Optimize and Save Animations

When you have created the frames for your animation and you are satisfied with the effect, you can optimize and then save the animation.

To maintain consistent color across all frames in an animation, use either the Adaptive, Selective or Perceptual color palette when creating your GIF optimization settings.

1 To optimize an animation, choose Optimize Animation from the Animation palette menu. It is recommended to leave both Optimize By options selected to achieve the best quality optimization. Click OK.

2 Choose File>Save for Web & Devices. Select one of the Gif optimization settings from the Preset pop-up. Or create your own custom GIF settings.

3 To preview the results of the optimization settings for different frames in the animation from within the Save for Web & Devices dialog box, click the Previous/ Next Frame, First/Last Frame buttons, or click the Play button to play all frames.

4 Choose a browser from the Browser Preview pop-up from the bottom of the dialog box. The browser launches and the animation plays in the browser window. File format information and HTML code are displayed below the animation for information purposes. Close the browser.

5 To save the animation, choose File>Save Optimized As. Specify a location and a name for the file. The .GIF file extension is appended automatically.

Tweening

The Tween command allows you to create smooth animations by creating additional frames between existing frames in the animation. These in-between frames create smoother movement.

1 To tween a frame, first click the New Frame button to create a duplicate of the first frame. Make a change (for example, reposition an object) to the layer on which you are working.

2 Click the Tween button in the Animations palette, or choose Tween from the palette pop-up menu.

3 For Layers, select the Selected Layer option to vary only the currently selected layer in the selected frame, otherwise leave the option set to All Layers. Choose Parameters options to specify which elements you want to tween.

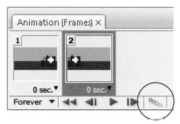

In this example it is important to choose Position, as it is the position of the layers in the animation that varies. Select Opacity and Layer Effects if these vary between frames.

4 Use the Tween with: pop-up to choose the frame with which you want to tween the currently selected frame. Enter a value in the Frames to Add: field to specify the number of in-between frames. The more frames you add, the smoother the animation, but you get a larger file size.

5 OK the dialog box. The in-between frames are added as new frames. Subsequent frames are renumbered accordingly.

Hot tip

The term "tweening" is derived from a traditional animation term "in betweening" where additional frames were created between key frames to create smooth animation effects.

Don't forget

Use tweening to dramatically reduce the amount of time needed to create smooth animations.

Don't forget

Tweened animation frames do not require a new layer for each new frame. The tweening effect takes place on an individual layer.

The Slice Tool

Slices are rectangular areas of an image that become the contents of a single cell in a HTML table, or that can be coded using Cascading Style Sheets. An image initially consists of a single slice by default, comprising the complete image. This becomes apparent when you select the Slice tool – a gray auto-slice icon () appears in the top left corner of the image. When you create a new slice, the remainder of the image is automatically divided into further slices.

You can create slices using the Slice tool, from ruler guides or based on layers.

Hot tip

As soon as you select the Slice tool, existing slices display automatically.

1 To create a slice using the Slice tool, click on the tool to select it. Position your cursor on the image, then drag to define the area of the slice. The slice you define is a User-slice.

2 When you release the mouse, Photoshop automatically generates additional slices for the remaining areas of the image which are not defined as User-slices. The additional slices are Auto-slices.

Hot tip

To use interactive alignment guides to align slices accurately, choose View>Show>Smart Guides. "Smart" alignment guides appear as you draw and move slices in an image with multiple layers and/or existing slices. To work effectively with smart guides, use them in conjunction with the Snap/Snap To options in the View menu.

3 Hold down Shift as you drag with the Slice tool for a square slice. Hold down Alt/option and drag to create a slice from the center out.

4 Choose View>Snap to>Slices if you want the Slice tool to snap to other slices or guides. The snap takes effect when your cursor comes within 4 pixels of a slice or guide.

228

Slices from Guides

A quick, convenient technique for slicing an image is to create slices based on ruler guides you position in the image.

1 Create or open an image. Drag in ruler guides to indicate where you want to create slices. (See page 23 for information on creating ruler guides.)

2 Select the Slice tool, then click the Slices From Guides button in the Options bar. The slices appear in the image. Each slice is numbered. Slices created from guides are User-slices. (See page 230 for information on User- and Auto-slices.)

3 To create a Layer-based slice, first select the layer in the Layers palette, then choose Layer>New Layer Based Slice.

Beware

When you use the Create Slices from Guides command, Photoshop deletes previously created slices.

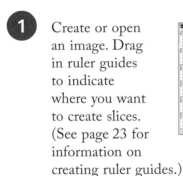

Don't forget

Slices you create using the Slices from Guides button, the Slice tool and the New Layer Based Slice command are created as User-slices.

229

User- and Auto-slices

Hot tip

User-slices have blue slice annotation symbols; Auto-slices have gray slice annotation symbols.

A slice can have one of two statuses: User or Auto. There are more possibilities for modifying User-slices. Slices you create using guides or the Slice tool are User-slices. Slices created automatically by Photoshop are Auto-slices. An image automatically consists of one Auto-slice comprising the full image.

You can change or "promote" an Auto-slice into a User-slice. This is useful as User-slices can be assigned different optimization settings. Auto-slices in an image are initially linked and therefore share the same optimization settings. The link symbol (🔗) that appears next to Auto-slices indicates that they share the same optimization settings.

Hot tip

You can promote a selected Auto-slice to a User-slice by clicking the Promote button in the Options bar:

There are two types of slices: Image or No Image. Image slices contain image information – pixels. No Image slices can contain a solid

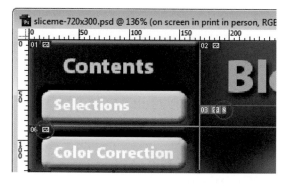

color, or HTML text. An Image slice is identified by the Image icon (🖼) when slices are visible.

Starting in the top left corner, slices are numbered from left to right and top to bottom. As you add, delete and rearrange slices, slice numbers update automatically.

Hot tip

To hide the display of Auto-slices, select the Slice Select tool, then click the Hide/Show Auto Slices button in the Options bar:

When selecting slices with the Slice Selection tool, User-slices are indicated by a solid boundary line and selection handles; Auto-slices by a dotted line.

Working with Slices

Use the following techniques to hide and show slices, and to manipulate them in a variety of ways.

1 To hide slices and slice information such as slice number and slice type icons, choose View>Show>Slices. To show slices, choose the same option again, or select either the Slice or Slice Select tool.

2 To select a User-slice, select the Slice Select tool. Click on a slice. A colored bounding box with eight selection handles appears around the slice indicating it is selected.

3 To move a slice, select the Slice Select tool, position your cursor within the slice you want to move and then drag the slice.

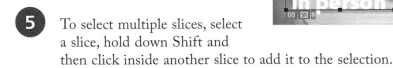

4 To resize a slice, select the Slice Select tool. Select a slice and then drag a side or corner resize handle.

5 To select multiple slices, select a slice, hold down Shift and then click inside another slice to add it to the selection.

6 To combine slices, first select two or more slices and then right-click (Windows), Ctrl+click (Mac) to access the context menu. Select Combine.

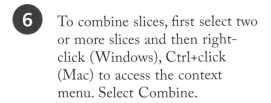

7 To divide a slice into multiple slices, either vertically or horizontally, select the slice, and then click the Divide button in the Options bar.

Hot tip

Slices show automatically when you select the Slice Select tool.

Hot tip

To delete a User-slice, first select it and then press the Backspace or Delete key. Auto-slices are automatically created to fill the same area.

Hot tip

To delete all User-slices in an image, choose View>Clear Slices.

Slice Options

The Slice Options dialog box enables you to set options such as URLs if you want to make slices into clickable buttons, as well as specifying whether slices are treated as an image or as an area to be filled with a background color or HTML text.

Don't forget

Photoshop can generate slices as a HTML table, or using Cascading Style Sheets. In the Save Optimized As dialog box (see page 209), click the Output settings button to specify which method is used.

1 To show the Slice Options dialog box, select a slice, then click the Slice Options button in the Options bar, or double-click inside the Slice.

2 The default slice name and slice number appear in the Name entry box. You can edit the slice name if required.

3 To make a slice a clickable button, enter a URL in the URL entry field. You should include the http:// specifier at the beginning of the URL for absolute paths.

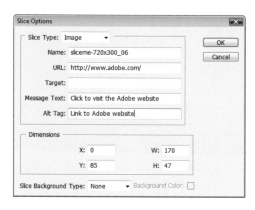

You can also specify relative paths. Enter the text you want to appear in the browser's status area and supply text for the alt attribute of the image if required.

Hot tip

When you assign a URL to an Auto-slice it becomes a User-slice.

4 Choose No Image from the Slice Type pop-up menu, then enter text in the text entry box. The text appears as HTML text in the area defined by the slice.

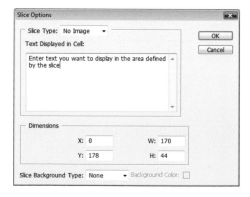

Beware

You cannot move or resize User-slices in the Photoshop Save for Web dialog box.

Optimizing and Saving Slices

When you finish creating and adjusting slices you can use the Save for Web & Devices dialog box to optimize and save individual slices, or complete images, for use on the Web.

Beware

Unselected slices in the Save for Web & Devices dialog box appear slightly dimmed to differentiate them visually from selected slices which appear as normal. This dimmed color overlay has no effect on the actual appearance or color values of the image.

1 To optimize slices in an image, choose File>Save for Web & Devices. Slice borders are visible by default. Click the Slices Visibility button in the toolbox on the left to hide/show slice borders as required. Select/deselect the Hide Auto Slices option in the Preview pop-up menu (>>) to control the visibility of Auto-slices in the dialog box.

2 To select an individual slice to optimize, select the Slice Select tool, then click into a visible slice in the optimized pane. The selected slice appears at full strength with a colored highlight border. To select multiple slices in order to apply consistent optimization settings, hold down Shift and then click into additional slices to add them to the initial selection, or drag through the slices you want to select with the Slice Selection tool.

3 To easily reselect related groups of slices, first select two or more slices, then choose Link Slices from the Optimize palette menu. The slice status icons appear in a different color to indicate the link.

...cont'd

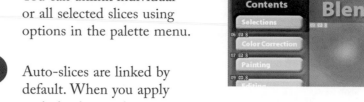

You can unlink individual or all selected slices using options in the palette menu.

Hot tip

Using the Slice Select tool, double-click on a slice to show the Slice Options dialog box.

4 Auto-slices are linked by default. When you apply optimization settings to an Auto-slice the settings apply to all Auto-slices. If required, you can select an Auto-slice, then choose Unlink Slice from the palette menu. This promotes the slice to a User-slice which you can then optimize with individual settings.

5 Create the optimization settings you require for each slice in the image using the Presets and/or the custom settings in the Optimization panel. (See pages 208–209 for further information on optimizing images.)

6 Click the Done button to return to the image, retaining any modified settings for the dialog box. Click the Save button to save the optimized slices.

Hot tip

To avoid the possibility of seams appearing between slices when optimizing using GIF or PNG-8 formats, make sure you use the same color palette and dither settings, especially for adjacent slices.

7 In the Save Optimized As dialog box select an option from the Slices pop-up menu. Choose Selected Slices if you selected specific slices prior to clicking the Save button and you do not want to save all slices in the image. (See pages 208–209 for further information on saving images.)

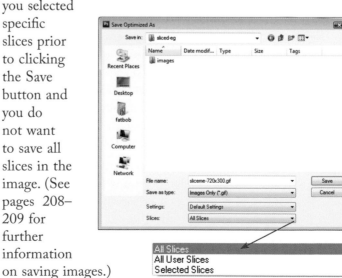

Index

M

N

O

P